The Agrarian Question in the Neoliberal Era

Primitive Accumulation and the Peasantry

Through the voices of the peoples of Africa and the global South, Pambazuka Press and Pambazuka News disseminate analysis and debate on the struggle for freedom and justice.

Pambazuka Press – www.pambazukapress.org

A Pan-African publisher of progressive books and DVDs on Africa and the global South that aim to stimulate discussion, analysis and engagement. Our publications address issues of human rights, social justice, advocacy, the politics of aid, development and international finance, women's rights, emerging powers and activism. They are primarily written by well-known African academics and activists. Most books are also available as ebooks.

Pambazuka News – www.pambazuka.org

The award-winning and influential electronic weekly newsletter providing a platform for progressive Pan-African perspectives on politics, development and global affairs. With more than 2,500 contributors across the continent and a readership of more than 660,000, Pambazuka News has become the indispensable source of authentic voices of Africa's social analysts and activists.

Pambazuka Press and Pambazuka News are published by Fahamu (www.fahamu.org)

Mwalimu Nyerere Chair in Pan-African Studies, University of Dar es Salaam – www.nyererechair.udsm.ac.tz

The Agrarian Question in the Neoliberal Era

Primitive Accumulation and the Peasantry

Utsa Patnaik and Sam Moyo
with Issa G. Shivji

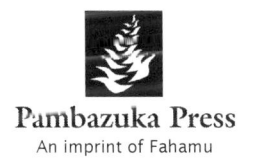

Pambazuka Press
An imprint of Fahamu

Published 2011 by Pambazuka Press and the Mwalimu Nyerere
Chair in Pan-African Studies, University of Dar es Salaam

Pambazuka Press, an imprint of Fahamu
Cape Town, Dakar, Nairobi and Oxford

www.pambazukapress.org   www.fahamu.org   www.pambazuka.org

Fahamu, 2nd floor, 51 Cornmarket Street, Oxford OX1 3HA, UK
Fahamu Kenya, PO Box 47158, 00100 GPO, Nairobi, Kenya
Fahamu Senegal, 9 Cité Sonatel 2, BP 13083, Dakar Grand-Yoff,
Dakar, Senegal
Fahamu South Africa, c/o 19 Nerina Crescent, Fish Hoek, 7975 Cape Town,
South Africa

Mwalimu Nyerere Chair in Pan-African Studies, University of Dar es Salaam
PO Box 35091, Dar es Salaam, Tanzania

http://nyererechair.udsm.ac.tz

© Mwalimu Nyerere Chair in Pan-African Studies, 2011

The right of Utsa Patnaik, Sam Moyo and Issa G. Shivji to be identified
as the authors of this work has been asserted by them in accordance with
the Copyright, Designs and Patents Act 1988.

All rights reserved.
No part of this book may be reproduced or transmitted in any form
or any manner, electronic or mechanical, including photocopying, recording
or by any information storage and retrieval system, without written
permission from the publisher.

British Library Cataloguing in Publication Data
A catalogue record for this book is available from the British Library

ISBN: 978-0-85749-038-4 (Pambazuka Press paperback)
ISBN: 978-9987-9418-1-0 (Mwalimu Nyerere Chair paperback)
ISBN: 978-0-85749-039-1 (ebook – pdf)
ISBN: 978-0-85749-040-7 (ebook – epub)
ISBN: 978-0-85749-041-4 (ebook – Kindle)

Manufactured on demand by Printondemand-worldwide

Contents

About the authors — vi

Preface — 1
Issa G. Shivji

Part 1 The agrarian question in the neoliberal era — 7
Utsa Patnaik

1. Introduction — 8
2. Advanced country living standards and developing country lands — 14
3. Was there an agricultural revolution in England? — 20
4. The fallacy of Ricardo's theory — 28
5. The unacceptably high cost of free trade — 34
6. The new primitive accumulation and the land question today — 47
7. Concluding remarks — 50

Notes – Part 1 — 54
Bibliography – Part 1 — 54
Annex – Part 1 — 57

Part 2 Primitive accumulation and the destruction of African peasantries — 61
Sam Moyo

8. Introduction: a failed agrarian transition in Africa — 62
9. Primitive accumulation by dispossession in colonial Africa — 64
10. Primitive accumulation and expanded reproduction? — 67
11. Recent land grabs and subordination of peasantries — 73
12. Alternatives during the neoliberal crisis — 79
13. Conclusion — 81

Note – Part 2 — 82
References – Part 2 — 82

Index — 86

About the authors

Utsa Patnaik has taught economics at Jawaharlal Nehru University, India since 1973 after completing her doctoral thesis at Oxford University. She has edited and co-edited several volumes including *Agrarian Relations and Accumulation – the Mode of Production Debate* (1991), *The Making of History – Essays Presented to Irfan Habib* (2000) and *The Agrarian Question in Marx and his Successors* in two volumes (2007, 2011). She has authored several books including *Peasant Class Differentiation – A Study in Method* (1987) *The Long Transition* (1999) and *The Republic of Hunger and Other Essays* (2007).

Sam Moyo is executive director of the African Institute for Agrarian Studies (AIAS), based in Harare, Zimbabwe, and has worked on rural development issues focusing on land reform, agrarian change, environmental questions and social movements. He is currently the president of CODESRIA. His key books include *The Land Question in Zimbabwe* (1995), *Land Reform Under Structural Adjustment in Zimbabwe* (2000), *African Land Questions, Agrarian Transitions and the State: Contradictions of Neoliberal Land Reforms* (2008). His co-edited books include most recently *Reclaiming the Nation: The Return of the National Question in Africa, Asia and Latin America* (2011).

Issa G. Shivji is one of Africa's leading experts on law and development issues. He is a prolific writer and researcher, producing books, monographs and articles, as well as a weekly column printed in national newspapers. Issa Shivji presently occupies the Mwalimu Julius Nyerere Research Chair in Pan-African Studies of the University of Dar es Salaam. Most recently, he has been working on the political economy of economic reforms in Tanzania. His publications include *The Concept of Human Rights in Africa* (1989), *Silences in NGO Discourse: The Role and Future of NGOs in Africa* (2007), *Pan-Africanism or Pragmatism: Lessons of the Tanganyika–Zanzibar Union* (2008) and *Where is Uhuru? Reflections on the Struggle for Democracy in Africa* (2009).

Preface

Issa G. Shivji

'It's a mad scramble for African farmland right now,' said Carl Atkin, who heads research at Bidwells Agribusiness, a large British company. The company was involved in recruiting investors at a first-of-its kind conference, held in New York in June 2009 and attended by institutional investors potentially interested in investing in Africa (Silver-Greenberg 2009). A study of five African countries – Ethiopia, Ghana, Madagascar, Mali and Sudan – in 2009 documented that over 6 million acres of land had been allocated to investors (the study only documented allocations of around 2,500 acres and over). Elsewhere on the continent, there have been the same stories of hundreds of thousands of acres being alienated to so-called investors. Encouraged and protected by their governments, a number of large agribusiness multinationals have been involved in 'land grabbing'. One report says that some 125 million acres (roughly equal to Sweden) have been grabbed by rich countries for outsourcing agricultural production to supply food to supermarkets in the West, Gulf countries, or even Africa itself (to cater for the burgeoning expatriate and elite markets). As one author puts it:

> Visit a supermarket in Abu Dhabi and you'll be greeted by row after row of picture-perfect produce ... It's likely those rows of shiny vegetables and fruit came from an improbable source: Ethiopia, a country practically synonymous with famine. Yes, Africa where one in three people is malnourished, is now growing tomatoes and butter lettuce for export ... (Mukherjee 2010: 53)

Growing food for export to take advantage of rising prices is the typical advice given to hungry Africa by the corporate world and their allies, the international financial institutions and western governments, including the so-called philanthropy houses such as the Bill and Melinda Gates Foundation. Together with the Rockefeller Foundation, the Gates Foundation launched the Alliance for a Green Revolution in Africa (AGRA) in 2006, whose avowed aim is to eradicate hunger in Africa 'through promotion of rapid, sustainable agricultural growth based on smallholder farmers'. In reality its programme is not based on smallholder farmers at all; rather, it rides on their backs to make profits for agribusiness and promote genetically modified organisms (GMOs), which are strongly advocated by the US through USAID. AGRA promotes the industrial agriculture model, based on intensive technology, use of chemical fertilisers, herbicides, pesticides and high-breed seeds, just as with the 'old' Green revolution in Mexico and India, which had ruinous effects on the environment and smallholders while benefiting big farmers and the rich peasantry. The new element in the 'new' Green Revolution is genetically modified seeds, produced by the world's most notorious seed multinational companies such as Monsanto. Directly and indirectly, AGRA is connected with transnational agribusiness corporations and biotech lobbies such as Africa Harvest Biotech.

As Bereano and English (2010) show, the Gates Foundation is linked in various ways to multinationals and biotech research organisations through the movement of personnel ('the revolving door') and grants and funding, all of which are promoting new technologies at a grand profit to some while their long-term effects on human health, biodiversity and indigenous agriculture systems are not known – although what is known shows that their effects can be disastrous. 'Over 165 examples of such contamination occurred in 2005–07 alone – by pollen flow, the careless escape of GE [genetically engineered] seeds, etc – resulting in hundreds of millions of dollars in damages' (Bereano and English 2010: 48) Powerful corporations, of course, were able to obtain compensation in out-of-court settlements, but African farmers have neither the political clout nor the finance to get a penny of compensation, although they are the biggest victims.

Besides the usual western suspects, companies from the newly emerging countries such as India, China and South Korea are also involved in land grabbing. These 'emerging countries', as the mainstream parlance goes, cannot, perhaps, be categorised as imperialist or sub-imperialist (Amin 2011) but they are certainly in the game. World hegemonies are changing and shifting and all these countries, whether established or emerging, are deeply involved in capitalist accumulation.

The latest phase of capitalist accumulation is characterised by the domination of finance capital. This is not the finance capital resulting from the merger of industrial and bank capital that Lenin talked about at the turn of the last century; it is, rather, the finance capital where the circulation of money dominates, determines and directs the circulation of commodities. Money, a means of exchange and a store of value, has turned into value itself. Money makes more money even though it is not tied to production of commodities. The classical formula, M-C-M$^+$ (money-commodity-more money) is turned on its head: M-M$^+$ (money-more money, without producing any commodity). In the classical Marxist language of political economy, exchange value is delinked from use value.

Thus it was that the leading banking houses of the world showed great liquidity when their assets consisted only of sub-divided mortgages, futures and financial securities. When the crunch came, and commodity eventually caught up with money, the financial architecture collapsed like a pack of cards. Liquid banks were actually bankrupt banks – their wealth consisted of values in the account books, with nothing to show for it on the ground.

The problem/crisis was systemic. It could not be resolved by tampering and tinkering. But unwilling and unable to face it as a systemic issue, the state, dominated by financial oligopolies, pumped in trillions of dollars of people's money – the so-called stimulus packages – to bail out the very banks that had caused the problem in the first place. Stimulation may have provided a temporary respite, but the crisis refuses to go away. Are the newly created, potentially endless wars (Libya, for example) the new stimulus package to save moribund capitalism? If so, it will not be for the first time.

In the history of capitalism, destruction and devastation (including wars) have been an innate part of its growth and development. After all, at every stage of its five-century history, the iron law of capitalism has invariably held: accumulation at one end and pauperisation at the other. The continent which has witnessed the greatest devastation in this process of worldwide capitalist accumulation is undoubtedly Africa. In Asia domestic industries were destroyed, resources pillaged and the people harnessed to the chariot wheel of accumulation in the metropoles. In North and Latin America, the Caribbean and Australia, the people were exterminated and their lands forcefully settled by the 'surplus' populations (meaning the unemployed, the poor, convicts) of Europe, released in their millions by the march of industrialisation.

In its encounters with Europe over five centuries, Africa went through all this and much more. Its people were turned into chattels and commodities to be sold and bought in their millions. The continent was depopulated of its youngest and most energetic. They were dehumanised, their social fabric and cultures destroyed and their humanity trampled on. The continent has yet to recover fully from the gruesome period of the triangular slave trade: African diasporas are found all over the world – African-American, African-Caribbean, African-Brazilian – and they still live in the most inhuman conditions. In the richest country of the world, you have a black man in the White House while thousands of black men are robotised to kill in its war machinery, the army, and hundreds are narcotised in its prisons.

In this book, Utsa Patnaik and Sam Moyo tell us of how the voracious appetite of globalised, neoliberal capitalist accumulation is being consuming the small producers of the periphery, the peasantry. This new phase of capitalist accumulation, based on the old form of accumulation – you could call it primitive accumulation or accumulation by dispossession – is rooted in the destruction of people and their livelihoods and the pillaging of resources: land, forests, minerals, water, bioresources. The trajectory of capitalist accumulation in the *longue durée* shows that primitive accumulation is not only a phase in, or original form of, accumulation, but rather lies at the very heart of the world system of capitalism. Devastation, pillage, destruction, wars and dehumanisation are inherent in the system. In relation to ecology and the environment, some have gone even further. They have argued that the Cartesian dichotomy between nature and human, between environment and society, is false and that the destruction of the environment is constitutive of the system, the capitalist system. In the current phase of neoliberal accumulation, as Patnaik and Moyo show, that form of accumulation is being visited upon the peasantry of the periphery, and even more or so in Africa, with a vengeance. Thus it emerges that, from the perspective of human history, the capitalist system itself is primitive. The choice before humankind, therefore, is not so much between capitalism and socialism, but rather between socialism and barbarism, as Samir Amin has so stubbornly argued over the years.

As humanity stands at the crossroads, where the choice is between rescuing the primitive system of capitalism, which will inexorably lead to self-destruction, or dumping it into the dustbin of history and building an alternative humane world, the question before us in Africa is: where do we stand?

Dar es Salaam
March 2011

Selected bibliography

Amin, Samir (2011) *Long Road to Socialism*, Dar es Salaam, Mkuki na Nyota and Mwalimu Nyerere Chair

Bereano, Philip L. and English, Travis M. (2010) 'Looking in a gift horse's mouth', *Third World Resurgence*, 240–41

Cotula, L.,Vermeulen, S., Leonard, R. and Keeley, J. (2009) *Land Grab or Development Opportunity? Agricultural Investment and International Land Deals in Africa*, Food and Agricultural Organisation of the United Nations (FAO), International Institute for Environment and Development (IIED) and International Fund for Agricultural Development (IFAD)

Harvey, David (2003) *The New Imperialism*, Oxford, Oxford University Press

—— (2005) *A Brief History of Neo-liberalism*, Oxford, Oxford University Press

Moore, Jason W. (2011) 'Transcending the metabolic rift: a theory of crises in the capitalist world-ecology', *Journal of Peasant Studies*, 38(1): 1–46

Moyo, Sam and Yeros, Paris (eds) (2005) *Reclaiming the Land: The Resurgence of Rural Movements in Africa, Asia and Latin America*, London, Zed Books

Mukherjee, Ananya (2010) 'The wrongs about the right to food', *Third World Resurgence*, 240–41.
Patnaik, Utsa (2007) *The Republic of Hunger and Other Essays*, New Delhi, Three Essays Collective
Rodney, Walter (1973) *How Europe Underdeveloped Africa*, Dar es Salaam, Tanzania Publishing House
Shivji, Issa (2009) *Accumulation in an African Periphery: A Theoretical Framework*, Dar es Salaam and Harare, Mkuki na Nyota and African Institute of Agrarian Studies
Silver-Greenberg, Jessica (2009) 'Land rush in Africa', Bloomberg Businessweek, 25 November, http://www.businessweek.com/magazine/content/09_49/b4158038757158.htm, accessed 6 May 2011

Part 1
The agrarian question in the neoliberal era

Utsa Patnaik

1 Introduction

It is indeed a privilege to have been asked to share with you some thoughts on the agrarian question in this, the momentous 50th year of the achievement of effective self-governance. The leader of Tanzania's freedom struggle, Mwalimu Julius Nyerere, was a towering personality who left the imprint of his egalitarian and socialist ideas not only on Tanzania but on Africa and the developing world. I feel doubly privileged to be with you during the Julius Nyerere Intellectual Festival Week. The struggle that colonised people waged was not for political independence alone, but also for a more just and egalitarian society, without which sovereignty cannot be sustained in the long run and in a real sense. That sovereignty is once more under attack in the current era of neoliberalism, and a new phase of struggle is necessary to preserve and enhance the gains of freedom.

The ascendancy of finance capital since the 1980s means that financial interests have come to dominate policymaking in the present era, both at the global level and through international financial institutions directing pliant governments, in almost all developing countries as well. The major pillars of neoliberal policies are: first, the imposition of deflationary cut-backs in state spending in nation states; second, openness of developing countries in particular to trade and capital flows through dismantling trade barriers; third, the dismantling, in developing countries only, of all price support mechanisms which existed earlier for stabilising prices for peasant producers, who constitute a large or major segment of the population; and fourth, a sustained attack on peasant-owned or -occupied land in the name of 'development'.

These policies have been adversely affecting the livelihoods and access to basic needs of millions of poor people, who make up the majority of the population in the global South. The agrarian depression, which has turned into a crisis in many areas, is hardly mentioned in the critiques mounted of the neoliberal agenda, even by progressive writers. There is a deep theoretical failure in understanding the links between the agenda of finance capital, on the one hand, and the agrarian crisis in developing countries, on the other.

Yet history tells us that a deep financial and economic crisis has never occurred without a prior agrarian crisis, which tends to last even after the financial crisis abates. Consider the great depression of the inter-war period: it started not in 1929 as the conventional dating would have it, but years earlier from 1924–25 when global primary product prices started steadily falling. The reasons for this, in turn, were tied up with the dislocation of production in the belligerent countries during the war of inter-imperialist rivalry, the First World War of 1914–18. With the sharp decline in agricultural output in war-torn Europe there was expansion in agricultural output elsewhere which, with European recovery after the war, meant over-production relative to the lagging growth of mass incomes and of demand in the countries concerned. The downward pressure on global agricultural prices was so severe and prolonged that it led to the trade balances of major producing countries going into the red.

Then, as now, the wrong policy advice was given by the centre of financial power, the British Treasury, that the way to tackle external imbalance was to deflate the economy – to reduce the level of activity by strongly cutting back budgetary spending by governments (Kindleberger 1987). We know today, after the theoretical labours of Keynes and Kalecki, that if one country does this it might benefit, but if all countries do it then it simply reduces aggregate demand in each country, reduces each country's demand for other countries' exports, and creates a deflationary spiral in which unemployment rises and the level of activity measured by output, as well as the extent of trade, reduces. The deep crisis this caused in the capitalist system, particularly in the late-industrialising countries such as Germany, Italy and Japan, led to belligerent militarisation as a 'solution', in which the size of armies ballooned and resources of other countries were forcibly seized for industrial 'development', leading to atrocious massacres and genocide. 'Civilised' Europe descended to a level of barbarism on a scale that the world had never seen before.

In the current era, it seems that no lessons have been learnt from history. In the last 40 years, global primary product prices saw one episode of sharp decline in the first half of the 1980s, exactly at the time that many African as well as Latin American countries started on IMF-guided 'stabilisation' and debt-conditional 'structural adjustment' programmes. Once again, recalling the 1920s and the British Treasury, the modern centres of financial power, the US Federal Reserve, in close consultation with the Bretton Woods institutions, misguidedly advised developing countries to strongly follow expenditure-deflating macroeconomic policies combined with free trade. The results have been extensively documented: owing to public expenditure cuts, there was decline in growth rates of investment and social sector outlays; stagnation or even – as in many African countries – absolute decline in per capita GDP took place; there was a big setback to campaigns for improving health and literacy; and food security was severely affected (Cornia et al 1987, Baker et al 1998).

After a period of rising primary product prices from the end of the 1980s to 1995, the capitalist world saw a second episode of sharp, primary price declines, this time a few years after India embarked on the same neoliberal policy path from 1991, and a decade after Africa and Latin America had already done so. This period, from the mid-1990s to the present, marks the agrarian crisis in Asia, which continues to immiserise large segments of its population. In India alone police records show that in the decade up to December 2008, 198,000 farmers had committed suicide, well in excess of 'normal rates' and mainly driven by debt. This is merely the tip of the iceberg. The agrarian crisis has contributed to the global financial and economic crisis and, in turn, has been further aggravated by it; but the existence and importance of the current agrarian crisis is not conceptually recognised by even progressive analysts in the South leave alone by the mainstream literature, nor are the links to the global financial and economic crisis ever discussed.

The questions I will try to take up are related to the contours of the current agrarian question in the neoliberal era. In what ways are the expenditure-deflating policies of finance capital to which I have already alluded affecting material output as well as aggregate demand of the agriculture-dependent population? Is there necessary benefit to both countries specialising and entering into free trade as Ricardian theory argues? How does trade liberalisation affect the peasantry of the global South? What is the meaning and consequences of the new surge of primitive accumulation on the part of local and global capital, which is seeking to separate the peasantry from land? And what is the way forward for resistance as well as reconstruction?

The peasantry of the global South is under historically unprecedented pressures today from attacks by capital not merely on its livelihood but also on the very means of securing that livelihood, namely the land it possesses. Recalling the primitive accumulation of capital which marked the birth and adolescence of capitalist production in Europe during the 16th to 19th centuries, we see once more, albeit in different forms and under different circumstances, a concerted attempt by global capital to acquire control, on the one hand over the use of peasant lands to serve its own purposes, and on the other hand, to seize that agricultural land itself for its multifarious non-agricultural purposes. But the 21st century is not the 18th or 19th century: the peasantry of the global South has nowhere to go to if it is dispossessed, in contrast to the dispossessed peasantry of the North, which migrated in vast numbers to the New World.

The peasantry today is turning from passive forms of resistance such as suicide to active contestation of the exercise of hegemony by global capital. This transition of segments of the peasantry from passive objects to active subjects of history marks an important and exciting moment of the current economic and political conjuncture. The present, acute global food crisis is a direct outcome of the new phase of attacks on the peasantry, which has been going on for more than three decades, but has escaped scholarly attention until very recently.

I do not agree with the basic premise articulated in the view that we are seeing the end of the classical agrarian question in the global South, its last stronghold, because capitalist accumulation within nations is no longer dependent on extracting the agricultural surplus. This view has been most clearly articulated by Bernstein (1996); it holds that the constraint on capitalist transformation imposed by a stagnant peasant agriculture has become unimportant and has been by-passed in the era of globalisation, since access to global capital flows allows development in poor countries without transfers of surplus from the domestic agricultural sector. The unquestioned premise in this argument is that it was in fact domestic capitalist transformation in agriculture which historically marked the rise in productivity in this sector and that through increasing domestic transfers of surplus, the successful industrialisation of today's advanced countries was achieved. A similar trajectory, now considered redundant, was expected for developing countries,.

However, a study of agricultural production and trade in today's advanced countries during their period of transition shows that far from this being the case, capitalist agriculture could not cope with the wage good (the basic necessities, such as food and cloth, bought by workers with their wages) and raw material demands of industrial transition and these demands were actually increasingly met by transfers from the heavily taxed peasantry and from the plantation agriculture set up in subjugated colonies. Productivity did rise in metropolitan centres but to an insufficient extent, making the industrialising countries increasingly dependent on primary sector imports. This proposition is explored in the third section of this paper through a study of the so-called 'agricultural revolution' in 18th to 19th century Britain.

Nor is it the case that today capitalist accumulation is globally independent of reliance on peasant agriculture. On the contrary, an even more intensive international division of labour is promoted vigorously, more far-reaching than that which prevailed in the earlier era of political subjugation. The entire thrust for free trade in agriculture, as promoted by the Bretton Woods institutions and through the World Trade Organisation (WTO), has as its primary aim the re-opening of the lands of the global South to meet the increasing demands of the North, while direct acquisition of land in tropical areas is also sought. Modern air-freighting has greatly extended the list of northern demands on southern lands, to include a range of perishable products, while governments are urged to facilitate the entry and functioning of the food business transnational companies.

Let us begin with a brief overview of the reasons for the linking of advanced country consumption patterns with the lands of today's developing countries.

2 Advanced country living standards and developing country lands

There is a widespread misconception that today's advanced countries had successful internal 'agricultural revolutions' which preceded or went ahead simultaneously with their industrialisation, and which provided all the necessary food, raw materials and energy for fuelling that process.[1] The misconception regarding successful 'agricultural revolution' has been assiduously promoted by historians in northern universities, ignoring the fact that there was very high import dependence for primary products on colonies and subjugated tropical lands from the very beginning of the transition in today's industrial Europe.

This was bound to be the case given the poverty of primary-sector production in northern countries, whose populations were in a miserable state before they acquired tropical colonies. The land was frozen or under snow for almost half the year. There was only one growing season and the need to grow fodder corps did not permit enough output of grains to maintain both human and animal populations, leading to slaughter of livestock at the onset of winter. B.H. Slicher van Bath, in his *Agrarian History of Western Europe* (1963), documents what he calls the 'extremely monotonous' and unhealthy diet of even the royal households of northern Europe in the 17th century – over 100kg of highly salted cattle and pig meat was consumed per head in the year, there were no produced sweeteners (natural honey was the main source), no fresh vegetables or fruit during the long winter months, while food was cooked using animal fats. The highly saline food – salt was a necessary preservative – produced 'an oceanic thirst' so that per capita beer consumption was 40 times higher then than today. Problems of hypertension, cardiac diseases and vitamin deficiency diseases plagued the population. Despite warm summers, ordinary people had to wear either woollen or leather clothing since body linen (linen is made from the fibres of the flax plant) was too expensive.

It was only after the North colonially subjugated today's third world regions, located in sub-tropical and tropical climes, and started slave-labour-based and later indentured-labour-based plantation systems, that the consumption basket of northern populations started to diversify and improve dramatically. Increasing imports made by the monopoly trading companies such as the East India Company, The Africa Company and the South Sea Company included cotton cloth, sugar, tea, coffee, tobacco, raw cotton, raw silk, vegetable dyestuffs, tropical cereals, natural fertiliser, tropical hardwoods and a host of other goods, none of which could be produced at all in northern Europe or, later, in North America. These are the crops mainly included in the B vector of crops in Table 1, which cannot be produced at all in cold lands. However, foodgrains, both wheat and rice, were also imported by European countries, including Britain, from their colonies.

Today, the list of demands made on southern countries by northern populations has become much longer, because while long sea journey times meant that only non-perishable goods could be imported, now modern air-freighting carries goods in a matter of hours to the other side of the globe. A very large range of perishable goods from fresh vegetables and fruits, vegetable oils, river and sea foods, to flowers and orchids are accessed from developing countries by the giant agribusiness corporations with their bases in advanced countries. They enter into contracts with local farmers or directly acquire land for production. The fresh vegetables and fruits today include not only tropical crops, which cannot be grown at all in cold lands, but also those crops that can be grown in cold countries but only in summer. Since they grow in winter in warmer developing countries, getting peasants there to grow these crops for export has virtually done away with the seasonal constraint on consumption for northern populations. Similarly, countries in the southern hemisphere which experience warm weather exactly when it is freezing in Europe are able to cater to seasonal demand.

Table 1 Comparing the range of primary products in the North and South

A larger and qualitatively different range of primary products are producible in the ex-colonised tropical developing countries than in today's industrially advanced countries

(Northern hemisphere)	Winter season		Summer/monsoon season
Tropical developing countries	$(a_1, a_2, a_3, \ldots a_n)$	+	$(b_1, b_2, b_3, \ldots b_n)$
Temperate advanced countries	$(0, 0, 0, \ldots 0)$	+	$(a_1, a_2, a_3, \ldots a_n)$

Note: The a elements going in number from 1 to n refer to the typical field crops such as grain and oilseeds, tubers such as potatoes, and vegetables such as cabbages and carrots. These crops are all cultivable only in summer in cold northern countries, with zero output in the winter season. These same crops, however, can be grown in the winter season in large tropical developing countries. The b elements refer to the typical tropical crops (sugarcane, raw cotton and jute, tropical fruit and vegetables) which are cultivated in tropical countries during the summer/monsoon season (or all year round in the case of tea, coffee and hardwoods). These cannot be cultivated at all in cold temperate advanced countries.

Most people in the global South have very little idea how heavily dependent the standard of living in advanced countries actually is on imports from their own richer, botanically diverse lands. On the contrary, just as the customer in a shop pretends he does not require the goods he actually covets in order to drive down the price, advanced countries incessantly lecture developing countries, telling them that they are poor and advising them that they can only grow richer by exporting. In the economic literature the heavy, one-sided import dependence of advanced countries on developing nations is completely ignored. The reality is that if developing countries had actually been resource poor, they would not have attracted the acquisitive greed of the emerging merchant capitalists of today's advanced countries; the North would not have found it worthwhile to colonise the South. When traders became rulers, their home country reaped a bonanza by way of free imports, since the colonial goods were acquired by paying local producers out of the very same tax revenues they themselves paid in to the colonial state. The same acquisitive greed drives modern capitalism, which uses the ideology of free trade and seeks to subordinate the use of developing country lands to the maintenance and further enhancement of living standards in advanced countries. Without such access to developing country lands, the northern supermarket shelves would be denuded of many foods now considered as essential, and the standard of life would plunge back to near-medieval levels for northern populations.

W.A. Lewis puts forward in his 1978 Princeton lectures, later published as *The Evolution of the International Economic Order*, the standard thesis that

> in a closed economy the size of the industrial sector is a function of agricultural productivity. Agriculture has to be capable of producing the surplus food and raw materials consumed in the industrial sector, and it is the affluent state of the farmers that enables them to be a market for industrial products ... The distinguishing feature of the industrial revolution at the end of the eighteenth century is that it began in the country with the highest agricultural productivity – Great Britain – which already had a large industrial sector ... But countries of low agricultural productivity such as Central or Southern Europe, or Latin America, or China had rather small industrial sectors, and there it made rather slow progress. (Lewis 1978: 10)

Lewis goes on to give as an instance of the allegedly higher productivity in Britain compared to the tropics: 'the yield of wheat by 1900 was 1600lbs. per acre as against the tropical yield of 700lb of grain per acre' (1978: 14).

But there is a fallacy in such a comparison because 'productivity' – here land productivity is being talked about – has no meaning without a time dimension. Over one year, an acre of land in Britain may well have produced 1,600lbs of wheat, but it could produce nothing else since there was only one growing season in cold temperate lands. In the tropics crops can be produced all the year round. Over one year, an acre of land in the tropics produced not only 700lbs of grain but also a second crop – either another type of grain or cotton or vegetables, plus often, a third crop of gram (pulses) or lentils. The river delta areas in India grow today, and have always grown, two irrigated cereal crops plus a third crop of pulses, requiring less moisture, over a single year. Tropical land in 1900 was much more productive than temperate lands when 'productivity' per unit area is properly measured and compared over the same annual time period. Despite all technical change in the advanced countries, to this day India, with a much smaller cultivated area than the US, produces annually a larger total tonnage of cereals, root crops, oil crops, sugar crops, fruits and vegetables. The precise figures are 858 million tonnes in India and 676 million tonnes in the US in 2007, the latest year for which the data from the United Nations Food and Agriculture Organisation is available.

As for China, its even more intensive cultivation, developed over centuries, and consequent high land productivity were legendary; Britain's agricultural yields at that time, properly measured over the same production period, were pathetic in comparison. By 2007 China produced 1,308 million tonnes from an area substantially less than that of India and of the US. True, technical change in northern agriculture produced higher output per worker or per labour day, but only by substituting dead labour – machinery – for living labour, machinery which required large inputs of fossil fuels to run. The 'energy balance', or the amount of energy embodied in all inputs required to produce a given level of energy embodied in output, is to this day more unfavourable in temperate lands.

Although not just W.A. Lewis but most historians of the northern countries claim that the North underwent successful 'agricultural revolution' preceding their Industrial Revolution, this claim does not stand up to careful investigation. The northern industrialising countries were not closed economies but were aggressively open, engaging in wars amongst themselves to capture trade routes and competing to acquire political control over highly biodiverse tropical lands. Their relative success in acquiring such control explains the absence of an agricultural constraint to their industrialisation. In the next section we look in some detail at the case of food production in England, which is viewed as the most successful country in Europe to have undergone an agricultural revolution in the 18th century, associated with land enclosures and transition to large-scale capitalist farming.

3 Was there an agricultural revolution in England?

The variable which is quite crucial as an indicator of welfare and a measure of the success of agricultural revolution is the growth of the basic food staple crop in relation to population growth. The older Brownlee series of population for England and Wales was revised by Lee and Schofield (Schofield 1981) and the latter series and the index derived from it is shown for 1701 to 1801 as Index A in Table A1 in the annex. Maddison (2006) also presents some more recent estimates on population for scattered years starting 1700 and ending 1870, from which I have calculated the growth rate between 1700 and 1801 and interpolated the intermediate year values on the assumption of steady growth. Index B for England and Wales (E+W) has been derived from this series in the table.

The main difference between the two series is the somewhat higher population in the latter series, more so in the earlier years, which reduces the growth rate slightly compared to the first series. I have derived the Maddison series for Britain, namely England, Wales and Scotland (E+W+S), in the same manner, which is shown as Index C.

From Chambers and Mingay (1970) we derive the rise in cereal output in physical terms over the 18th century from their discussion that the area under wheat rose by a quarter and yield rose by about one-tenth while the rise in the non-wheat cereals was a somewhat faster. This broad picture is confirmed by later research (Overton 1996a and 1996b, Turner et al 2001 – though Brunt 1999 suggests a somewhat higher rise). This gives an increase of 37.5 per cent for wheat and 43 per cent for all cereals over the period 1700 to 1800. I distributed the increase of 43 per cent over the decades of the century in the same proportion as total agricultural output value is distributed in Cole 1981. This is a better procedure than to distribute the increase assuming a constant growth rate.

This exercise gives us the index of cereal output shown in the first column of Table A2 in the annex.

We can check that per capita cereal output declines for every population index, by varying degrees, the largest decline being by 17.4 per cent using the Lee and Schofield index, with the Maddison indices giving around 13 per cent decline. The Lee and Schofield population series is the only complete one and the Maddison population figures are only for individual years at the beginning and end of the century, with values I interpolated by assuming a constant growth rate of population, which was not actually the case. The per capita cereal output Index A, using the Lee and Schofield series, should be regarded as the better approximation to the actual trends. This shows that per capita output rose slowly up to the mid-18th century (and this is consistent with the small net export of corn[2] which existed up to 1770). After 1750, however, per capita cereal output starts declining and despite slight recovery by 1780, the decline resumes in the last two decades coinciding with war.

It should be noted that a 17.4 per cent decline is quite substantial, given that the initial level of availability itself was low. This is confirmed when we study wheat or corn, the major food staple of the population. We rely on the absolute estimates of wheat area, yield and output given by Turner, Beckett and Afton (2001) for 1750 to 1850, which are reproduced in Table A3. I have also incorporated in this table the rise by 25 per cent in area and of yield by 10 per cent that Chambers and Mingay (1970) mention over the entire century, to derive the 1700 figure of output. This gives a total rise of output from 33.41 to 45.94 million bushels or by 37.5 per cent, whereas population increased by 73.2 per cent on the Lee and Schofield figures (Schofield 1981) and by 64.7 per cent on the Maddison (2006) figures.

The authors are sanguine about per head output and thought that on the whole, English agriculture continued to feed the larger population adequately. They support the Overton (1996a, 1996b) position that agricultural revolution was a reality in the 18th century. This conclusion however is contradicted by Overton's own statement:

Population grew at an average of 0.26 per cent per annum from 1700–1750 whereas all the agricultural output indices grew more rapidly (ranging from 0.38 to 0.60 per cent per annum): *from 1750–1850 population grew at an average of 1.07 per cent per annum and the estimates of agricultural output ranged from 0.77 to 0.82 per cent per annum.* (Overton 1996a – emphasis added)

On the basis of every revised series of population, it is obvious that not only wheat but also per-head agricultural output declined between 1750 and 1800 and remained stagnant between 1800 and 1820. It appears from the above statement that the subsequent rise was not enough to recover the lost ground and on balance per capita output remained lower in 1850 than a century earlier. This is also the finding of recent detailed research with time series data for the period, even after allowing for a possible substantial margin of error (see Allen 1998, 1999, Clark 2002). The interesting point is that the decline is concentrated in the second half of the century onwards, when the maximum 'improvements' were taking place with the transition to capitalist agriculture. From Table A4 the annual compound rate of net output growth for wheat over the entire 18th century works out to 0.32 per cent, with the first half registering 0.31 per cent and the second half 0.325 per cent. This rise in the growth rate of net output is so insignificantly small in the second half of the century, the difference being only 0.015 per cent, that it could not cope with the acceleration in the rate of population growth, and per head net output fell.

The annual per capita output in bushels is converted to kilograms for comparison with present-day levels in developing countries in Table A4. The initial level of 140kg per capita, virtually unchanged taking 1700 and 1750, is itself extremely low. If we accept from the writings of contemporaries and those who have investigated diet composition, that at least three-fifths of the population relied on wheaten bread (while the remainder consumed other grains), then the per capita figure for the wheat-dependent population, is raised to 233kg in the mid-18th century. This is still quite low and compares poorly with many Asian and North African developing countries today, such as Indonesia and Egypt, whose grain consumption out of domestic output in 2007 was 250kg and 358kg respectively (Food and Agriculture Organisation, Rome database).

By 1800 per capita wheat output was down to an astonishing low of 111kg. Owing to cropping pattern and dietary changes, two-thirds of the population is estimated to have become dependent on wheaten bread. (This seems too low and is probably obtained by including the Irish population, which subsisted on potatoes, but which should not be counted when we are considering the grain output of England and Wales). Per capita availability from domestic production for them would thus have been at most 168kg only by 1800 and remained unchanged in 1820. So effectively the decline would have been from 233kg to 168kg for the wheat-dependent population or by 28 per cent. Given the inequality in the distribution of incomes, the quantities affordable by the labouring poor would have been much lower; little wonder then, that they rioted for cheap bread. It remains to be worked out what the situation for those dependent on rye, oats, potatoes and the like would have been.

Domestic production can be augmented by imports, and actual availability is given by domestic output plus net imports. But as we know imports were artificially restricted by the Corn Laws and the absolute quantities imported were kept so low that they had a negligible impact in raising availability, right up to the 1820s. From Table 2 we see that from exporting grain in the first half of the 18th century, by the end of the 1760s net exports became negligible and the direction of the import–export balance was reversed. Net grain imports started and grew slowly but steadily from the beginning of the 1790s. Imports doubled by the decade 1810–19 and again by 1830–39 to 1.3 million quarters or 16,230 tons. From Figure 1 we see that as domestic per head output fell the net imports start rising. However, this figure must be read carefully as the variables are plotted on different axes, and the absolute import figures translate into an amount per head which was quite trivial and would have raised availability by about one kilogram annually for the wheat-consuming population by 1820.

The failure of agricultural revolution in the 18th century to raise output sufficiently was compounded by the import restrictions on grain. Together they produced a period of acute stress for the bulk of the population, which was obliged involuntarily to

Table 2 Annual average net imports of wheat and wheaten flour into England 1720-29 to 1880-89

Decade	Net wheat (corn) imports in thousand quarters* (M − X)	Decade	Net wheat (corn) imports in thousand quarters* (M − X)
1720-29	-105.5	1810-19	662.9
1730-39	-296.7	1820-29	814.7
1740-49	-289.3	1830-39	1298.4
1750-59	-312.8	1840-49	1782
1760-69	-138.5	1850-59	3240
1770-79	-43.1	1860-69	5844
1780-89	-23.4	1870-79	9160
1790-99	324.5	1880-89	11372
1800-09	580.9		

* 1 quarter = 28 lb, so 4 quarters = 1 cwt = 112 lb

Source: Annual series on exports and imports in Mitchell and Deane (1962) up to 1820-29 in thousand quarters. From 1820-29 to 1885-89, five-year averages from Hobsbawm (1967), in units of 10,000cwt, were converted to units of one thousand quarters and ten year averages taken in order to splice the series with the first series.

consume less. The rise in rent and profits in this period came primarily out of food price inflation, which led to a redistribution of income away from net food purchasers and towards the foodgrain producers and sellers, as well as towards all employers of wage-paid labour, who experienced a profit inflation.

It is only from the 1830s that imports start growing a little faster, and they take off after the repeal of the Corn Laws in 1846. From below 2 million quarters at the time of repeal, imports trebled over the next two decades and reached 12 million quarters by the 1880s.

In 18th-century England, there may well have been a revolution in the social relations of production, but the resulting capitalistically organised agriculture showed little success in meeting

Figure 1 Annual imports of wheat (decade averages) 1720-1889, in thousand quarters

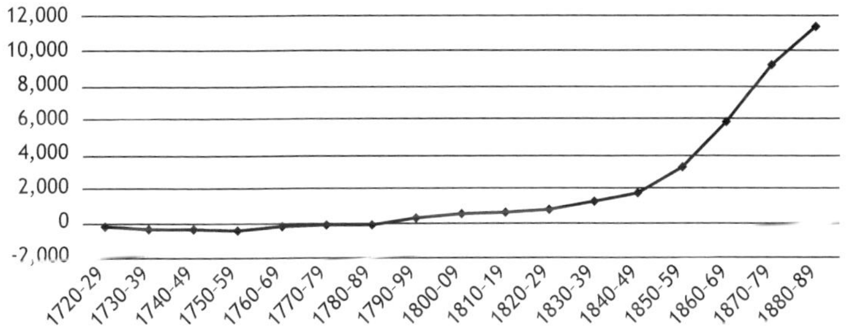

Source: Table 2

the challenge of industrialisation from the point of view of raising the productivity of land and labour to the extent required. After 1750 despite all 'improvements' and even though the area planted expanded, yields actually declined resulting in hardly any rise in the rate of foodgrains output growth, which fell below population growth, leading to a substantial decline in per head output for the population dependent on wheat, the major food staple. Food supply did constitute a serious bottleneck to the growth of the factory system, which could expand only at the expense of a severe reduction in the living standards of workers, leading to political unrest and prolonged agitation for free food imports. Britain's subsequent increasing dependence on foodstuff imports, to the extent that imports exceeded domestic supply, did not constrain its balance of payments or curb the second phase of industrial development. However, this was only owing to the very special nature of the interaction between the trade that Britain carried on with its colonies, much of which was transfer, and its trade with the rest of the sovereign world. This interaction requires further investigation.

I have argued elsewhere that the term 'agricultural revolution' in today's advanced countries can hardly be applied, for agricultural productivity did not rise sufficiently to meet the wage-goods needs, let alone raw materials. The first industrial nation, Britain suffered a food deficit by the 1790s even before the first phase of the Industrial Revolution had got under way, and only increasing food imports from its nearest colony, Ireland, and food and raw material imports from its tropical colonial possessions in the West Indies and India, allowed its industrial transition to proceed at all.

The long-term annual growth rate of basic cereal output in Britain was only 0.27 per cent between 1750 and 1850, well below the population growth rate, entailing falling per capita output and necessitating imports (Patnaik 1992). These imports would have been even higher if landlords had not obstructed imports by enacting the Corn Laws in order to protect their high rents. The 1790s in England saw repeated food riots by the urban labouring poor protesting against the high price of bread. The most important and well-documented agitation on a political economy issue was the prolonged 50-year struggle for the abolition of the Corn Laws and for cheap bread. David Ricardo wrote his 'The Effects of a Low Price of Corn on the Profits of Stock' in 1815, but the campaign did not succeed until 1846, when all tariffs were finally abolished.

What does the prolonged agitation for free food imports indicate but the total failure of domestic capitalist transformation of agriculture to meet basic foodgrain needs from internal production? The situation would have been even grimmer without the ability to exploit Ireland. By 1800 the colonised Irish population, ground down under heavy rents and taxes, was made to contribute 11–18 per cent of total consumption of wheat, meat and butter in England – thus most of urban consumption came through imports (Jones 1981). Further, the main raw material of the Industrial Revolution, raw cotton, was entirely imported since cotton did not grow in Britain. By the 1840s Britain was importing substantially more primary products by constant value than it produced itself (Davis 1979). This was only possible because most of the imports were costless to the country as a whole – they were 'paid for' to colonised producers out of the taxes these same producers were made to contribute, or they represented the commodity form of slave rents or peasant rents.

To this day, for several vital consumption items, the landlocked countries of industrial Europe import several times more than they can domestically produce, while for spices and non-alcoholic tropical beverages their import dependence approaches infinity since domestic production is zero.

4 The fallacy of Ricardo's theory

Ricardo's theory of comparative advantage is incorrect for it contains a fallacy, namely the 'converse fallacy of accident'.

The developing countries are urged to 'open up' their agriculture to free trade and the theoretical rationale put forward continues to be David Ricardo's theory of comparative advantage, based on the two-country, two-commodity model. This famous argument, where Ricardo took England and Portugal as the two countries and cloth and wine as the two commodities, said that even if the second country, Portugal, could produce both goods more cheaply than the first country, as long as the relative cost of production was different – namely one country, say Britain, by producing one unit less of wine could produce more of cloth than could the other country – then it would make economic sense for Britain to specialise in cloth and Portugal in wine. For unchanged total output of one good, the output of the other good would increase through such specialisation, and by trading both countries could then consume more of one good for no lower consumption of the other good – thus both countries would benefit. This was put forward as the incentive for countries to trade with each other and at the same time it was claimed to be the actual outcome of such trade.

Extremely clever though the argument is, it is logically incorrect. Ricardo's formal process of inference is correct, but the assumption that 'both countries produce both goods' is wrong – it is an incorrect statement of fact and therefore the argument contains a material fallacy. When the assumption is incorrect then the inference that trade is mutually beneficial does not follow and the entire theory becomes invalid. It is most unfortunate that an incorrect theory has been taught for two centuries and continues to be taught uncritically to this day.

Figure 2 Types of fallacies in argument

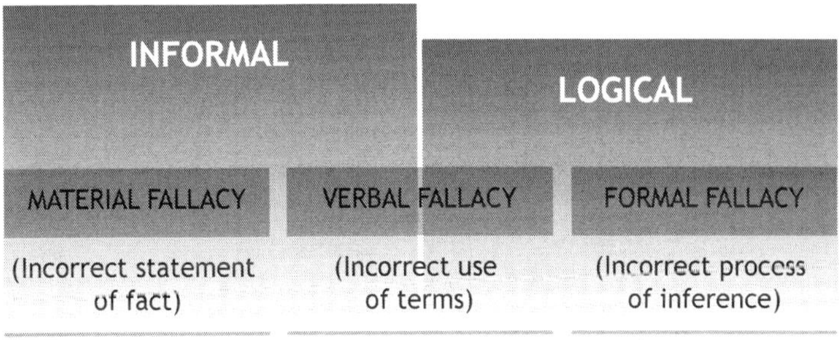

INFORMAL		LOGICAL
MATERIAL FALLACY	VERBAL FALLACY	FORMAL FALLACY
(Incorrect statement of fact)	(Incorrect use of terms)	(Incorrect process of inference)

Fallacies can be of several types – material fallacies arise from incorrect statement of fact, verbal fallacies arise from incorrect use of terms, and formal fallacies arise from an incorrect process of inference. Logicians classify the material and verbal fallacies, taken together, as 'informal fallacies' as contrasted with formal fallacies, while the verbal and formal fallacies taken together are logical fallacies as opposed to the material fallacies (since both verbal and formal fallacies arise in discourse or in logos as opposed to the world of matter).

Ricardo starts with a highly specific and restrictive assumption – 'both countries produce both goods' – and from this specific assumption improperly reaches a general conclusion that mutual benefit follows from specialisation and trade. 'Both countries produce both goods' is a crucial assumption, for without it, relative cost advantage cannot be defined or obtained. Unless there is positive output for both goods in each country, we cannot say how much of good 2 each country can produce by shifting to it the resources released by reducing output of good 1 by one unit, and compare these figures. But we have already seen that it is a materially incorrect assumption since Table 1 holds and a large range of primary products cannot be produced at all in cold temperate lands that import these products.

The strange thing is that Ricardo's own example does not satisfy his own assumption – grape wine could not be commercially produced in Britain, which was too cold to grow grapes. Even if the specific example is modified – as Paul Samuelson does without explaining why – to 'food' and 'cloth' instead of the original 'wine' and 'cloth' it does not rescue Ricardo's theory from its materially incorrect assumption. In most cases of the trade of developed countries with developing countries, his assumption is not satisfied.

If, say, Tanzania exports coffee to Germany and imports machinery from it, the standard economist's formulation would be that this occurs because Tanzania has a 'comparative cost advantage' in producing coffee while German's 'comparative cost advantage' lies in machinery. But this is a nonsensical statement, for it necessarily assumes that Germany can produce both machinery and coffee, which is untrue. In reality the output of coffee in Germany is zero and no figure of cost of production, leave alone relative cost, can be derived. If coffee output in Germany is zero and will always be zero, obviously we cannot say how much machinery can be produced by shifting resources out by reducing coffee production by one unit, and compare it with the figure for Tanzania.

The specific form of material fallacy into which Ricardo falls is the 'converse fallacy of accident'. The fallacy of accident arises when a general premise is applied to a specific situation where the premise does not hold. An example is the statement 'All persons can see. Homer is a person. Therefore Homer can see.' The 'accident' of Homer being blind makes the inference a false one. The converse fallacy of accident as the term suggests, improperly argues from a specific case to a general conclusion, which is thus asserted to hold even in the cases where the assumption is not true. Taking the same example, the converse proposition 'Homer is blind. Homer is a person. Therefore all persons are blind,' represents the converse fallacy of accident. From a highly specific case, an improper generalisation is made, so the inference 'all persons are blind' is not true. Similarly, from the highly specific assumption 'both countries produce both goods' an improper generalisation was made by Ricardo that specialisation and exchange benefit both parties to the trade. This inference is not true because the assumption is not satisfied – a major part of global trade volume was and continues to be in the primary commodities of warm lands which cannot be produced at all in the North. A numerical example to show that mutual benefit does not follow when one country cannot produce both goods, is available in my essay 'Ricardo's Fallacy' (Patnaik 2005).

We can visualise Ricardo, like any other civilised gentleman in England at that time, drinking a cup of Caribbean slave-labour produced imported coffee sweetened with imported cane sugar while smoking imported tobacco, with a carafe of imported grape wine at his side – since none of these four goods could be produced in cold Britain. He is wearing a shirt made from imported cotton – a raw material not producible in his country – while sitting at a polished mahogany table – an imported tropical hardwood not producible in Britain, and writing with ink containing imported dyestuff. We might ask him why, when his own experience blatantly contradicted it, he made the assumption that 'both goods are produced in both countries', to draw the fallacious inference that specialisation and trade were always mutually beneficial, namely not only did Britain benefit but so did slaves in its Caribbean plantations and heavily taxed peasants in India. Why it was necessary for Britain to use gunboats to blast open foreign ports, to militarily subjugate other peoples in order to impose free trade if it was indeed so beneficial for these people, is a question which is never posed.

That an incorrect theory should have enjoyed such an long innings in economics has to do with the important apologetic role it has played and continues to play in justifying as mutually beneficial all those trade patterns which were in reality the outcome of the exercise of military and political power. Whatever Ricardo's own views may have been, his theory has lent itself to being used to argue that specialisation and trade are always beneficial to both parties even when this was clearly not the case.

Scholars from developing countries themselves have been completely hegemonised ideologically by Ricardo's theory, and in defiance of the historical experience of trade-led decline in welfare and even famines in their own countries, have compounded the original fallacious reasoning which led Ricardo to draw the incorrect inference of mutual benefit from trade. W A. Lewis in

The Evolution of the International Economic Order (1978) put forward a modified Ricardian theory of comparative advantage to fallaciously 'explain' why the North developed while what he calls 'Chinese coolies' and 'Nigerian peanut farmers' remained poor. This is based on his notion of the product wage, namely the idea earlier stated by him that the tropical farmer produced much less grain than did the temperate land farmer because yield per unit area was higher in the latter.

As we have already seen, this idea of lower land productivity in tropical lands is not correct. The precise definition of 'land productivity' is important, for it has no meaning without a time dimension, and in this respect the definition is not spelt out by Lewis. While a hectare of land in the wheat belt of Canada or the USA grows one wheat crop alone over a year and nothing else, since the ground is frozen for half the year, a hectare of land in the Indian Punjab over a year grows wheat, cotton and sometimes an oilseed; a hectare of land in delta areas of South India grows two crops of rice and a crop of groundnut or pulses. A unit of land in the Mekong delta in Vietnam can grow eleven crops over four years. The Nigerian farmer produces not only grain but also cotton and coffee.

The combined output of the two to three crops that a hectare grows annually in a tropical land is the correct output to compare with the output of the single crop grown annually in the cold temperate land. Land productivity properly measured with a uniform time dimension is far higher in tropical lands. The basic argument Lewis puts forward on what he called the 'factoral terms of trade' is thus factually unsound:

> A farmer in Nigeria might tend his peanuts with as much diligence and skill as a farmer in Australia tended his sheep but the return would be very different … the market price gave the Nigerian for his peanuts a 700 lbs.-of-grain-per-acre level of living, and the Australian for his wool a 1600 lbs.-per-acre level of living … because these were the respective amounts of food their cousins could produce on their family farms. (Lewis 1978: 21–2)

But in fact more food could be produced over a year in Nigeria and at a lower cost per unit of output than in Australia, so the explanation based on food output for Nigerians being poorer than Australians cannot be correct. What is missing from the entire discussion is that the settler population in Australia represents out-migrating Europeans, mainly Britons, while the population in tropical Nigeria is a colonised or ex-colonised black population, historically subjected to tax-financed and hence unrequited exports to Britain. Australians produced, exported and got paid for their exports, while Nigerians were taxed by Britain, with the commodity-equivalent of taxes being exported.

It does not strike W.A. Lewis, or most modern writers, that developing countries are poor today precisely because they were, and are, much richer in primary resources than today's developed countries, which in the past made every effort to acquire control and continue to depend to this day, more and more heavily, on these developing countries for their food, beverages, fibres and energy.

5 The unacceptably high cost of free trade

A study of history proves irrefutably that, far from benefiting both parties, trade in primary products entailed extremely heavy costs for the exporting country because it led to decline in the output and availability of basic food staples for its own population and in many cases even led to famine, with large-scale mortality. The inverse relation – between rising agricultural exports and falling domestic foodgrains availability – is repeatedly seen not only in colonial times but in every case of the trade liberalisation of a developing country.

A long decline in per capita foodgrain production and availability took place in India during the 50 years before independence. Production fell from 200kg around 1900 to a nadir of 136kg by 1946 entailing severe agrarian distress, falling mass nutrition, and famine in Bengal during 1943–44, which claimed over 3 million lives and reduced many millions more to destitution. After independence the agrarian economy was protected for nearly 40 years and output of foodgrains per head slowly climbed back to 183kg per head by the early 1990s. In the last 15 years of neoliberal deflation and trade liberalisation, however, the entire gain of these four decades has been wiped out and India is back to the per capita output level of the first plan period 1950–55. Availability per capita is even lower than output because substantial net exports continue as the downward shift of internal mass demand following from expenditure-deflating policies has been only partially reversed. In the current decade food output per head has been falling faster than ever before.

Building up the minimum conditions for food security is a long haul but destroying what has been built up takes little time, merely the dogmatic implementation of misguided policies. In sub-Saharan Africa, where the largest and most populous countries

Table 3 Decline in cereal and foodcrops output per head, sub-Saharan Africa, 1980-87/89

		Triennial average output			
1	**Six most populous countries**				
		1980	1981-83	1984-86	1987-89
	Cereals (million tons)	19.15	21.06	23.29	16.45
	Population (millions)	196.73	208.85	229.38	253.32
	Output per head (kg)	97.31	100.93	101.54	64.93
	Index	100.01	103.6	104.3	66.2
	Tubers*				
	Output per head (kg)	48.14	48.38	48.95	51.48
	Index	100	100.5	101.7	106.8
	Total food crops index	100	102.6	103.4	80
2	**Sahelian countries**				
	Cereals (million tons)	5.32	6.03	6.83	8.29
	Population (millions)	31.25	32.94	35.63	38.69
	Output per head (kg)	170.3	183	191.8	214.3
	Index	100	107.5	112.6	125.8
3	**All 46 countries**				
	Cereals (million tons)	37.51	40.7	44.6	40.25
	Population (millions)	349.75	370.62	406.17	450.45
	Output per head (kg)	107.2	109.8	109.8	89.4
	Index	100	101.5	102.4	83.4
	Tubers*				
	Output per head (kg)	31.26	37.81	36.83	33.07
	Index	100	120.9	118.1	105.8
	Total food crops index	**100**	**106**	**105.8**	**88.5**
	Per head (kg)	138.46	147.61	146.63	122.47

*Tubers include potatoes, cassava, yams, bananas and plantains. There was no recorded tuber output for the Sahelian economies.

Source: Calculated from crop and country-wise data in African Development Indicators 1992 (UNDP) Tables 1-1, 8-7. Published in Patnaik 1993.

followed intensive adjustment programmes along with freeing trade, the export crops grew at between 6 to 13 per cent annually while basic food staples either showed an absolute decline or grew below 2 per cent, leading to sharp fall in per capita food staples output.

Table 4 shows the estimated decline in per capita cereal output and per capita all food staples output in the six most populous countries of sub-Saharan Africa during the second half of the decade 1980–1990, when most of these countries were following intensive adjustment programmes, involving sharp cut-backs in state development spending, and opening up to free trade. Over the 1990s the decline per head in output continued, though at a slower rate. At the same time the exportable crops were growing annually between 6 per cent (Kenya) to 13 per cent (Sudan). Even after net food aid is included, five of the six most populous countries saw average per capita calorie intake decline for their populations as Table 4 shows, the only exception being Nigeria.

Why should there be a drastic slowing down of output growth for foodgrain crops as developing countries follow economic reforms and liberalise their trade? I have long argued that there is always such an outcome, resulting in an inverse relation between producing for export and maintaining domestic food availability. The reason is both simple at one level and profound at another. Land is not a product of human labour and has to be conceptualised as akin to fossil fuels since the supply of both is fixed. Nor is land homogeneous in its productive capacity since warm tropical lands produce, as we have seen, not only a far larger variety but a qualitatively different output mix compared to the cold lands of advanced countries.

The motive of acquiring control over tropical biodiversity was a major driver of the colonial subjugation of other nations by the West Europeans. By setting up slave-labour-based and later indentured-labour-based plantation systems, a steady stream of tropical primary consumption goods and raw materials was maintained both to diversify European diets and clothing, as well provide the raw material for the new industries. Moreover, most of this swelling flow of valuable goods was not paid for since local taxes were used to buy them or they embodied slave rent.

Table 4 Change in average per day per capita calorie intake in the six most populous African countries

Country	Cereal imports (000T) 1		Food aid cereals (000T) 3		Change in imports net food aid 5	% Change in calorie per head 6
	1980	1990	1979/80	1989/80	1980–1990	1979/81–1989/91
Tanzania	399	73	89	22	-259	-2.17
Ethiopia	397	687	111	538	-137	-9.92
Uganda	52	7	17	35	-63	-6.0
Nigeria	1828	502	–	–	-1326	15.45
Kenya	387	188	86	62	-175	-9.86
Zaire	538	336	77	107	-232	1.54

Source: P. Patnaik 1999: 174, using U. Patnaik 1993, various issues of the World Bank's *World Development Report* and the FAO, Rome, 'Food Balance Sheets 1992-94'.

The objective of promoting free trade under the International Monetary Fund–World Bank guided economic reforms, strengthened by the WTO discipline, has been to bring about a further intensification of the international division of labour in agriculture, where tropical countries are increasingly pressured to produce the relatively exotic requirements of rich advanced country populations, to keep the supermarket shelves in the North well-stocked with everything from gherkins and winter strawberries to edible oils and flowers. The resulting foodgrain deficits of developing countries, as they divert more land to export crops, are supposed to be met by their accessing the global market for grains, which is dominated by USA, Canada and the European Union, with Argentine and Australia as smaller players.

In country after country the idea of 'food security' was redefined by the international financial institutions pressing for free trade and internal economic reforms. Developing countries were told that in a modern globalised world 'food security', in the sense of aiming for self-sufficiency in foodgrains production, was outdated even for large countries with poor populations. Rather, developing countries would benefit from specialising in the non-grain crops in which they had a 'comparative advantage', by increasing their exports, and by purchasing their grain and dairy products requirements from northern countries which had a surplus of these products.

Developing countries were urged to dismantle their domestic systems of grain procurement and distribution at controlled prices, which most of them had put in place after decolonisation precisely in an attempt to break free from earlier colonial systems of specialisation and trade, which had severely undermined their nutrition standards. Historical memories are short, it would seem. Many developing countries, ranging from the Philippines to Botswana, unwisely dismantled their grain procurement and distribution systems in the decade from the mid-1990s.

The determined thrust by the advanced countries to 'open up' trade-protected economies in the global South, both under loan conditionalities and using the WTO discipline, received an added impetus from the loss of a substantial grain export market with the break-up of the Soviet Union after 1990 under conditions of economic collapse. By 1993 the cumulative loss of grain exports to this region was nearly 30 million tonnes and the search for alternative grain markets was stepped up. This was quite successful since a large number of developing countries, undergoing shifts in cropping pattern towards exports as mandated under trade liberalisation policies, became food import dependent to a greater or lesser extent over the next decade.

The model of export specialisation thrust on developing countries or unwisely adopted by governments was always at the cost of declining food security for the mass of the people. The promises of increased export earnings and ability to access food from global markets proved misleading and false even before the current inflation started. First, with dozens of developing countries following the same policies of exporting much the same products, the unit dollar price of their exports declined and terms of trade moved against them. A doubling of the volume of exports over a decade if accompanied by a halving of the unit export price means no increase in exchange earnings at all. Most developing countries altered their cropping patterns but ended up with little or no rise in export earnings. Second, even if foreign exchange is not a constraint, governments do not privilege the interests of the poor and in India there is official denial that hunger has increased. India has a mountain of foreign exchange, and restrictions have been removed on the free purchase of hard currencies by those rich enough to go on holidays to Europe or the US.

It is very clear by now that as regards the advanced countries' agenda of restoring the colonial-type trading patterns, there has been 'over-shooting': the decline in foodgrains output per head in the developing world has been far greater than the increase in developed countries, leading to an overall global decline in per capita output and availability by 2004. The 1980–85 per capita world cereal output of 335kg per annum declined to 310kg by 2000–05. Among developing countries China and India, which together accounted for over 30 per cent of world cereal output in the early 1990s, contributed significantly to global per capita output decline (FAO database).

Let us consider the following ten developing countries: China, India, Indonesia, Philippines, Vietnam, Iran, Egypt, Pakistan, Bangladesh and Sri Lanka, which together contributed 40 per cent of world cereal output. Over the 13-year-period and 1989/91 to 2003/04 we find a mere 15.6 per cent rise in aggregate cereal output from this group. That is a very small rate of growth, only 1.1 per cent per annum, well below the nearly 2 per cent population growth rate of these countries, and entails falling output per head. At the same time the output of their export crops has been rising fast, up to ten times faster than food crops output, owing to land and resources diversion to export crops.

The eight northern developed countries which together accounted for 56 per cent of world cereal output (US, Canada, UK, France, Germany, Netherlands, Italy and Spain) showed over the same period only an 18.6 per cent rise in cereal output, or an annual growth rate of 1.3 per cent, which was ahead of their own population growth, but insufficient to both meet their own rising domestic needs and provide an adequate surplus for trading with and meeting the increasing deficit of the developing world.[3]

The developing regions subject to such enforced exports suffered a decline in grain availability for the local population and falling nutrition, sometimes culminating in famine, as their limited land and resources were diverted to the export crops. For a brief period after decolonisation these countries privileged domestic food security and protected themselves from iniquitous international trade. Since the late 1970s, however, there has been a renewed onslaught by the advanced countries desiring access to the superior productive capacity of developing country lands, and owing to modern air freighting the range of products demanded has expanded manifold. While earlier only a few non-perishable products were traded (sugar, tea, coffee, timber, cotton) now a very large range of perishable goods, from fresh vegetables and fruit to flowers, are also demanded for stocking northern supermarket shelves in the depth of winter. The transnational agribusiness corporations have extended their tentacles into dozens of developing countries, either by using contract systems or by purchasing on the market, which transmits global price volatility into peasant agriculture. No mass peasant suicides owing to debt took place before 1991 in India. Since 1996 as global primary prices fell and under the WTO discipline, protection has been virtually removed; indebtedness-driven farmer suicides started from 1998. Total recorded farmer suicides between 1998 and December 2008 were 198,000; specifically debt-driven suicides have claimed over 60,000 peasant lives over the last decade.

The predictable result of more exports has been the sharp decline in foodgrain output for local populations that we have discussed so far. The colonised Indian peasant starved while exporting wheat to England and the modern Indian peasant is eating less while growing gherkins and roses for rich consumers abroad. The rapidity of the decline is explained by the fact that deflationary reform policies have also cut back public investment in agriculture at the very same time that they pushed more exports, so yield growth is falling and there is not the slightest possibility of maintaining both exports and domestic grain production from a total sown area which is constant.

In China, too, economic policies of trade liberalisation and an export thrust have entailed a very heavy cost by way of diversion of land (within a stagnant total sown area) to commercial crops, particularly to cotton for the rapidly expanding exports of textiles to the world. As a result despite its also being the world's largest importer of raw cotton, foodgrain area declined and the cereal output per capita fell sharply, even more sharply than in India, from 210kg to 168kg, over the period 1990/1–2003. Imports have not risen to compensate owing to rising unemployment and demand deflation reducing mass purchasing power. Given that a much larger share of the declining per head output is going as animal feed, the availability for the poorer mass of the population especially in rural areas is bound to have declined more sharply than the average. China's rural areas are in turmoil with nearly 80,000 cases of peoples' protests being registered annually.

Failure to understand the significance of foodgrain decline

Despite the severely adverse effects on food security, most economists remain conceptually blind to the per capita foodgrain decline, owing to a serious misconception they have regarding the behaviour of demand for cereals as a country's income rises.

John Maynard Keynes had remarked that the world is moved by little else but ideas. Once a wrong idea gets into the head of a policymaker it is very difficult to get it out. Keynes's argument on the paradox of thrift – if every person saves more, the nation ends up saving less – is still not understood 75 years after the *General Theory* and finance ministers continue to behave like housewives, cutting back spending to balance budgets even though they have to deal with rampant unemployment. Many ill-advised policies we see creating havoc around us arise from incorrect but obstinately held ideas.

The crucial incorrect idea here is that there is nothing surprising about cereal consumption falling – as a country develops and its per head income rises, people diversify their consumption away from 'inferior' cereals and towards 'superior' food, including milk, eggs, meat, and so on. Most economists thus believe in what they call a 'negative income elasticity of cereal demand', and this influences many others, so they actually interpret declining grain consumption in a positive light. Their idea, however, arises from ignorance and is factually incorrect. It represents a fallacy of composition, in which only a part of total cereal demand – that directly consumed (as boiled rice, chapatti and so on) – is taken into account, and cereal demanded as livestock feed converted to milk, eggs, meat, and so on is ignored. In fact diversification leads to a rise, not fall in the consumption of cereals or foodgrains.

Fifty years of data from the United Nations Food and Agriculture Organisation show that as average income rises in a country and diets become more diversified to superior foods, the per head cereal/foodgrain demand, far from falling, rises steeply, and average calorie and protein intake rise in tandem. This happens because much more cereals get consumed indirectly as feed converted to animal products. The feed demand not only rises, but rises steeply as per head income rises (other things, especially income distribution remaining the same). This steep rise occurs because of the high feedgrain-intensity of animal products, which, however, provide only about one-third to one-sixth of the calorie intake of the same weight of cereals.

Thus one kilogram of cereals consumed over a week provides a person with 3,460 calories energy and about 95–100gm protein. One kilogram of chicken meat provides much less energy, only 1,090 calories, but more protein at 258gm. A well-to-do person who prefers chicken and substitutes one kilogram cereal with chicken, would need to consume 3.2kg chicken meat over the week to maintain the same energy intake as before. This would require under Indian (and most developing country) technical conditions nearly 4kg of feedgrain since on average 1.2kg feedgrain is required to produce one kilogram of chicken meat. The same feed conversion factor is true of one litre of milk or one kilogram (or about 18) medium eggs.[4] Thus substituting chicken/milk/eggs for one kilogram of directly consumed cereal while giving unchanged energy intake to the consumer entails a rise in demand for cereals to as much as 4kg under developing country conditions (the conversion factors are higher in developed countries).

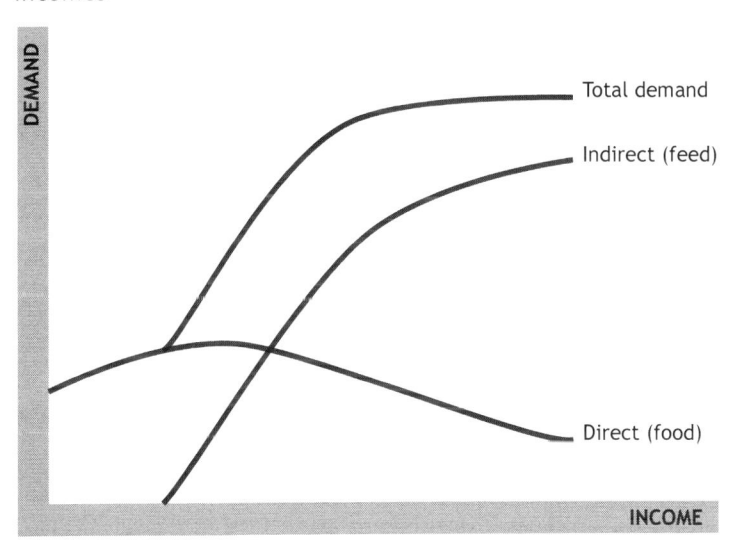

Figure 3 Direct and indirect demand for grain with rising incomes

Source: Yotopoulos 1985

As Adam Smith had pointed out two centuries ago, the cost of all agricultural products is determined by the cost of grain, since this is food staple or wage good for workers, and feed for working plough animals, as well as feed for obtaining livestock products. The substitution of working animals by machinery has altered only one component of these three.

Well-to-do consumers, as they diversify diets towards animal products, thus draw away larger and larger quantities of cereals from direct use to indirect use as feedgrain. A rich consumer can end up absorbing in a year, six to seven times the quantity of cereals that a poor consumer can afford. A poor person in India belonging to the bottom one-third of the population ranked by monthly spending is found to consume less than 100kg cereals annually, with only a twentieth of this being indirect consumption as animal products, while the richest urban consumer with a western lifestyle can easily consume 500kg annually, with the bulk of it being indirect consumption as animal products.

Pan Yotopoulos (1985) had presented this relation in a stylised form, shown as Figure 3. This represents the situation over time in a given country as its average income rises. It can also depict the cross-sectional picture at a given point of time, taking countries at varying levels of average income. There is a well-established international discourse around this relation. The higher the average income of a country, the higher is its cereal consumption and the higher the share of the latter that is indirectly consumed, as the figure shows. The richest country in the world, the United States, consumed nearly 900kg per head of cereals in 2007, of which only one-eighth was directly eaten and three-fifths used as feed converted to animal products, with the balance being processed. Its cereal consumption was more than five times higher than the 174kg recorded by India and its normalised calorie intake (namely, deducting 1,000 calories as survival level) was two and a half times higher than in India.

China has been raising its income fast and by now it converts a massive 115 million tonnes of cereal output as feed to animal products, compared with less than 10 million tonnes in India. Its people consume directly as much as Indians do, but owing to more diversified diets they consume nearly 300kg cereals per head, 115kg more than we do, and their average calorie and protein intake is higher. Particularly noteworthy is the fact that by 2007 India's consumption fell below the average for the African countries, as well as below the least developed countries. Owing to higher average direct consumption in India, however, its average calorie intake remained a little above the average of the least developed countries and of Africa.

Why has India's average consumption declined to such a low level despite rising average income? Since India and China have seen high growth rates, observers as disparate as Paul Krugman and George Bush explained the 2008 global food price rise in terms of fast-rising cereal demand in these countries. They were quite right to expect rising demand in India but quite wrong to

Table 5 Output and direct and indirect consumption of cereals, for selected countries/regions, 2007

Cereals
Quantity (million tonnes unless otherwise stated)

1 Country/region	2 Production	3 Net imports and stock changes	4 Total supply	5 Food (direct use)	6 Feed, seed, processing, other (indirect use)	7 Per head direct kg	8 Per head total, kg	9 Per cent of indirect to total
India	212.4	−9.5	202.9	177.7	25.2	152.6	174.2	12.4
Least developed	125.9	4.5	140.4	105.5	34.9	136.9	182.1	24.9
Africa	130.8	58.1	188.9	138.7	50.2	144.1	196.4	26.6
China	395.3	−8.9	386.4	203.8	182.6	152.5	289.1	47.3
European Union	261	14	275	61.7	213.3	125.1	557.3	77.6
USA	412.2	−137.6	274.6	34.5	240.1	111.6	889.5	87.5
World	2121.3	54.6	2066.7	966.2	1100.5	146.6	313.6	53.2

Source: 'Food Balance Sheets' from FAO. Break-up of indirect uses into feed, seed, processing and other, available in source, which gives data up to 2007, www.faostat.org/site/368/DesktopDefault.aspx?PageID368

think it had actually happened. The observed decline in food supply and demand, which over the last decade has pushed India below Africa and the least developed countries, is not normal for a country with rising average income, and has resulted from the lopsided, inequitable nature of growth.

Krugman and others did not take account of the adverse changes in income distribution, owing to severely income deflating fiscal policies advised by the Bretton Woods institutions and faithfully implemented by successive Indian governments after 1991, which sent agriculture in particular into a depression from which it has still not recovered. With unemployment rising, with the fruits of growth going to a tiny minority while the masses suffered income deflation, the effects of dietary diversification by the rich have been swamped by an absolute decline in cereal intake for the majority.

National Sample Survey (NSS) data show for all except two states an absolute fall in average animal products intake as well, along with falling direct cereal intake over the reform period. No wonder average energy and protein intake have both fallen. People other than the rich are not diversifying diets; even the hungry are forced to cut back and are suffering nutritional decline.

By 2008, the situation was even worse, despite good output. A record 31.5 million tonnes of foodgrains were exported plus added to stocks, reducing domestic cereal supply steeply to 156kg per head, substantially lower than the least developed countries. This happened because the global recession raised unemployment and food prices spiralled to lower real incomes, so there was a fresh round of loss of purchasing power. While the least developed countries and African countries are internationally recognised as food insecure, and food is imported, the perception for India is totally at variance with the reality of increasing hunger. For one thing, India's high GDP growth rate is wrongly interpreted as benefiting everyone whereas it has benefited a minority. For another, official poverty estimates show a misleading decline in poverty, and few people realise that this decline is statistically spurious since it is the result of steadily lowering the standard against which poverty is being measured.

6 The new primitive accumulation and the land question today

The classical land question, far from being superseded or rendered irrelevant by the new globalisation, today explicitly occupies centre-stage among all issues of political economy precisely because of the upsurge of the new globalisation, which involves a new thrust to acquire control over tropical land. The earlier era of globalisation was imperialism in the direct and naked form of political control, wrested by force by a handful of advanced countries over mainly tropical countries and hence over their natural resources. The land of colonised countries, with their highly diversified crop production capacities, their mineral and forest resources, their vast gene pool of flora, were all directly controlled and became indispensable not only for sustaining the high living standards of populations in northern lands but also enabled, through unrequited exports, industrialising countries to finance capital exports to the regions of European migration.

After decolonisation an interregnum followed, ranging for different countries from two to four decades starting from the 1950s and 1960s, when the newly independent developing nations tried to follow a relatively autonomous trajectory of development in order to reverse the earlier decline in living standards of their own populations. This necessarily meant a certain degree of delinking from the earlier international division of labour. The very success of this delinking on the part of the oil-rich developing nations in particular led to a crisis for the advanced industrial economies which heralded a revival of the ideological dominance of financial interests from the late 1970s. Within a few years it has also led to a revival of imperialist adventurism vis-à-vis oil-rich nations, and to a backlash in the form of terrorism.

47

For the majority of the countries of the global South, however, renewed dominance of financial interests and its policies in the core capitalist countries has meant that there is a renewed attempt to control the use of their land, mineral and other primary resources, through the promotion of an economic 'discipline' of free trade, free capital flows and domestic fiscal contraction. It is an interesting fact that under the regime of free and volatile capital flows, India has recently seen large capital inflows which are not justified by its small current account deficits. It is unable to absorb the inflows by quickly expanding its level of economic activity owing to the simultaneous operation of fiscal 'discipline' that even amounts to contraction. Thus capital inflows simply add to reserves, which are then mainly held in dollar-denominated assets. Much of the capital inflow is debt-creating flows, which means that India is borrowing short at high interest rates and lending long at much lower interest rates – lending mainly to the USA through its investment in US Treasury bills. This difference in earnings amounts on various estimates to at least 2 per cent and up to 4 per cent of Indian GDP and this is one way in which a transfer is taking place.

The global capitalist system has been reeling from crisis to crisis over the last three decades and there is considerably enhanced insecurity of lives in the core capitalist countries. The problem of greatly enhanced capitalist instability is not confined to financial crisis: it originated in the real economy and in turn has had severely adverse implications for the employment and livelihoods of ordinary people. A prolonged agrarian crisis from the mid-1920s heralded the collapse of the pre-First World War global capitalist system during the inter-war depression. The agrarian crisis was characterised by falling primary product prices, peasant pauperisation and demand deflation throughout the capitalist world while only the socialist Soviet Union grew fast. Similarly, a prolonged global agrarian depression has heralded the current financial and economic crisis, the difference being that farmers in developing countries are now the worst affected, since the advanced capitalist countries are today much richer and their farmers receive large subsidies calibrated to the external environment.

Having itself created a situation of simultaneous output deceleration and deficient global demand for the masses through its implacable agenda of macroeconomic contraction, finance capital is obliged to seek other modes of expanding its sphere of activity. The late 19th century saw both a long depression and the age of high imperialism in which hitherto 'unoccupied' parts of the South were carved up and occupied by the leading capitalist powers.

Today, as the internal springs of capitalist expansion at the core dry up, we see another offensive to acquire the energy, mineral and other primary resources of the global South by the capitalist powers, which now include the East Asian late-industrialisers. The local corporate sector enters into collaboration with the giant transnational companies in this new process of primitive accumulation. This process has been variously called 'accumulation though encroachment' and 'accumulation through displacement'. Such a process of displacement of peasants from their land is also very clearly visible in China but for different reasons, because for nearly the last three decades official policy has encouraged private profit seeking and the exclusion of earlier egalitarian policies.

7 Concluding remarks

I have argued elsewhere that the principal contradiction is shifting rapidly in the agrarian sphere to that between the peasantry and workers on the one hand and imperialism with its local landed collaborators on the other. Many people in the left who are not familiar with the idea or analysis of contradictions feel alarmed because they think that 'the land question' is being put on the back burner. Nothing could be further from the case: they should remember that when the principal contradiction shifts to that between all the toiling masses and imperialism, it means that this contradiction is the one, 'whose existence and development determines and influences the existence and development of all other contradictions' (Mao Zedong n.d.) including what was earlier the principal contradiction.

There is a direct onslaught today on peasant and tribal resources, both land and water, by the corporate sector. The restrictions on landownership by non-cultivators, where they existed, have been removed by state governments, and ceilings on landholdings have been rolled back in many states to facilitate the entry of agribusiness corporations. The peasantry is losing land against debt on a massive scale and despite asset loss is getting pushed further and further down into the mire of hunger. Even the former rich peasants and surplus producers are facing steeply falling profitability and have started leasing out land on hunger rents to dispossessed peasants. The earlier phase of capitalist development in agriculture in India, marked by the rise of capitalist farming from within the peasant classes, as well as the emergence of landlord capitalism, has virtually ended owing to the steeply falling profitability of direct capitalist cultivation. Reverting to extracting surplus through land rent and usurious interest is once again the order of the day, and peasant pauperisation is seen once more.

The clearest indicator that the principal contradiction is

changing is provided by the very fact of the agrarian crisis itself, which in its scale, generalised nature affecting all the peasantry and its depth is quite unprecedented. This ongoing crisis is the direct outcome of the implementation of the neoliberal reform policies and trade liberalisation detailed above. In short it flows from the impact of imperialist globalisation on the agrarian sector combined with the state facilitating land grabbing by the international and national corporates.

The corporatisation of agriculture, which is promoted by the government, represents the control of transnational capital over our peasant production, and not 'the development of capitalism in agriculture', which has a completely different connotation in Marxist-Leninist literature. The 'development of capitalism in agriculture' took place when expansionary policies of autonomous national development were followed as during 1950 to 1990 in India, and it was geared to an expanding internal market. It led to some prosperity, though very unequally shared, in the agrarian sphere. By contrast the corporate subjugation of peasant production is nothing but the imperialist domination of our peasantry for the purpose of export production and it pauperises the peasantry and labourers.

The giant transnational corporations entering our agriculture today tie peasants to contracts under debt by way of advances of high-tech genetically modified (GM) seeds and inputs. When in general profitability is falling because prices on global markets are low, these corporations set the terms of contract in such a way as to grind the peasants down to sub-human levels of living because they ruthlessly seek to maximise their own profits. The experience of other countries in Latin America and sub-Saharan Africa has demonstrated this clearly, as has the experience of growers of coffee, tea and other export crops in Kerala, who are losing land against debt and committing suicide.

Thus the land question has now become one of defending the right of peasants, including tribal peoples, to their land and livelihoods. Not only can it never be separated from the fight against imperialist globalisation, this fight is a necessary condition for any advance on the land question. It is shameful that no resistance has been articulated by the liberal intelligentsia and political movements to the modification of ceiling laws or the permission for non-agriculturists to acquire land, all for the benefit of corporations. There is no outcry against blatant usury or land loss against debt, whereas even the colonial period saw anti-usury laws and enactments against peasant land alienation as a result of debt.

The minerals-rich areas of India, for example, are mainly forested areas inhabited by tribal populations. The wholesale acquisition of extracting rights over coal, iron ore and precious metals by foreign companies and local corporate houses through agreements signed with local state governments involves substantial displacement of tribal people and settled peasantry alike, who are now resisting such acquisition. The complete failure of prospects for alternative employment and of alternative livelihoods today means that the loss of land assets or forest rights will not be tolerated by the affected people. This is in contrast with the relative absence of protest in the phase of land acquisition for industry or mining in India after independence, when an expanding economy offered much better prospects for absorbing the displaced.

Moreover, the worst effects are yet to be seen, for today there is a determined effort being made by the advanced countries, supported by their local collaborationists, to acquire direct control over land and water resources through contract farming, to enmesh our farmers in high-tech debt through GM seed and plants, and to acquire control over the genetic basis of our biodiversity and over water resources through privatisation of water. In this they are aided by the collaborationist elements in key decision-making positions in government, and they also have the support of collaborationist elements among the domestic landlords.

The solution lies first in economic strategies for restoring the viability of small-scale production and second, it lies in forging the political unity of the small-scale producers and the working class to resist eviction and displacement from the land. Both are difficult tasks but are by no means impossible. Restoring the viability of small-scale production requires voluntary cooperation among them in a myriad ways ranging from pooled investment efforts to common marketing arrangements. Only cooperation can overcome the problems of small scale and strengthen the bargaining power of producers on the market, and many models of voluntary cooperation are already emerging. The question of displacement from their resources by the corporate sector, which has become an acute one in many Asian countries in particular, cannot ever be resolved by pitting the rural and tribal small producers against the working class, as is being attempted by some resistance movements in India. These issues of displacement have to be thrashed out on the basis of the striving for unity between small producers and working class movements against corporate land grabbing and acquisition without adequate compensation. Only the combative unity of all the affected peasant classes and workers against the onslaught of imperialism and its domestic collaborators can salvage the situation of progressive asset loss suffered by the small producers and increasing incidence of hunger in the global South.

Notes – Part 1

1. For the standard exposition of 'agricultural revolution' in Britain, see P. Deane 1969, P. Mathias 1969 and J.D. Chambers and G.E. Mingay 1970.
2. In British English, 'corn' refers to the chief cereal crop of a district, which in England was usually wheat.
3. Only Argentina, Brazil and Australia taken together show a large rise of 72 per cent in cereal output or an annual growth rate of 4.5 per cent over the period, but their combined weight at below 6 per cent of global output is too small to outweigh the deceleration in the major producing areas.
4. The calorie, protein and fat intake of different food items is provided in every five-yearly report of the National Sample Survey (NSS), entitled 'Nutritional Intake in India'.

Bibliography – Part 1

Allen, R.C. (1998) 'Agricultural output and productivity in Europe, 1300–1800,' University of British Columbia, Department of Economics Discussion Paper 98
—— (1999) 'Tracking the agricultural revolution in England', *Economic History Review* 42(2): 209–35
Aristotle *De Sophisticis Elenchis* (Of Sophistical Refutations, from Organon), in Barnes, J. (ed) (2004) *Collected Works of Aristotle*, vol.1, Princeton, NJ, Princeton University Press
Baker, D., Epstein, G. and Pollin, R. (1998) *Globalization and Progressive Economic Policy*, Cambridge, Cambridge University Press
Bernstein, H. (1996) 'The agrarian question then and now', *Journal of Peasant Studies*, 24(1–2)
Blyn, G. (1966) *Agricultural Trends in India 1891–1947*, Philadephia, PA, University of Philadelphia Press
Brunt, L. (1999) 'Estimating English wheat production in the Industrial Revolution', University of Oxford Discussion Papers in Economic and Social History no.29, June
Chambers, J.D. and Mingay, G.E. (1970) *The Agricultural Revolution 1770–1850*, London, Batsford
Clark, G. (2002) 'The Agricultural Revolution and the Industrial Revolution: England, 1500–1912', www.econ.ucdavis.edu/faculty/gclark/papers/prod2002pdf, accessed 15June 2010
Cole, W.A. (1981) 'Factors in demand', in Floud, R. and McCloskey, D.N. (eds) *The Economic History of Britain since 1700, vol.1 1700–1860*, Cambridge, Cambridge University Press
Cornia, G.A., Jolly, R. and Stewart, F. (eds) (1987) *Adjustment with a Human Face*, vol.1, Oxford, Clarendon Press
Davis, R. (1979) *The Industrial Revolution and British Overseas Trade*, Leicester, Leicester University Press

PART 1

Deane, P. (1969) *The First Industrial Revolution*, Cambridge, Cambridge University Press

Floud, R. and McCloskey, D.N. (eds) (1981) *The Economic History of Britain since 1700, vol. 1 1700–1860*, Cambridge, Cambridge University Press

Hobsbawm, Eric (1967) *Industry and Empire*, London, Penguin

Kindleberger, C.P. (1987) *The World in Depression 1929–1939*, London, Penguin

Jomo, K.S. (ed) (2006) *Globalization under Hegemony*, Oxford, Oxford University Press

Jones, E.L. (1981) 'Agriculture', in Floud, R. and McCloskey, D.N. (eds) *The Economic History of Britain Since 1700, vol.1 1700–1860*, Cambridge, Cambridge University Press

Kula, Witold (1976) *Economic Theory of the Feudal System*, London, New Left Books

Lewis, W.A. (1978) *The Evolution of the International Economic Order*, Princeton, NJ, Princeton University Press

Maddison, A. (2006) *The World Economy: vol. 1 A Millennial Perspective; vol. 2 Historical Statistics*, Paris, OECD Publishing

Mao Zedong (n.d.) *Selected Works*, Beijing, Foreign Languages Publishing House

Mathias, P. (1969) *The First Industrial Nation*, London, Methuen

Mitchell, B.R. and Deane, P. (1962) *Abstract of British Historical Statistics*, Cambridge, Cambridge University Press

National Sample Survey Organisation, India (NSS) (2003) *Income, Expenditure and Productive Assets of Farmer Households*, Report 497

Overton, M. (1996a) 'Re-establishing the English Agricultural Revolution', *Agricultural History Review*, 44(I): 1–20

—— (1996b) *The Agricultural Revolution in England*, Cambridge, Cambridge University Press

Patnaik, P. (1999) 'The pitfalls of bourgeois internationalism', in Chilcote, R.M. (ed.) *The Political Economy of Imperialism*, Oxford, Kluwer Academic

Patnaik, U. (1992) 'Was there an agricultural revolution in England?', paper presented at the School of Oriental and African Studies, University of London, July. Revised version presented to the Indian History Congress, Delhi, May 2010

—— (1993) 'The likely impact of economic liberalisation and structural adjustment on food security in India', paper presented at seminar organised by the National Commission for Women, India and the International Labour Organisation, New Delhi, January

—— (1996) 'Export oriented agriculture and food security in developing countries and India', *Economic and Political Weekly*, 31(35–37), reprinted (1999) in *The Long Transition – Essays on Political Economy*, Delhi, Tulika

—— (2003a) 'On the inverse relation between primary exports and domestic food absorption under liberalized trade regimes', in Ghosh, J. and Chandrasekhar, C.P. (eds) *Work and Wellbeing in the Age of Finance*, Delhi, Tulika

—— (2003b) 'Global capitalism, deflation and agrarian crisis in developing countries', Social Policy and Development Programme, paper no. 13,

United Nations Research Institute for Social Development (UNRISD), October
—— (2003c) 'Food stocks and hunger – causes of agrarian distress', *Social Scientist*, 31(7–8) July–August
—— (2005) 'Ricardo's fallacy', in Jomo, K.S., *Pioneers of Development Economics*, Delhi, Tulika
—— (2006) 'The free lunch – transfers from the tropical colonies and their role in capital formation in Britain during the Industrial Revolution', in Jomo, K.S. (ed) *Globalization under Hegemony*, Delhi, Oxford University Press
—— (2007a) *The Republic of Hunger and Other Essays*, Delhi, Three Essays Collective
—— (2007b) 'Neo-liberalism and rural poverty in India', *Economic and Political Weekly*, 28 July–3 August
—— (2011) 'The "Agricultural Revolution" in England', in Moosvi, S. (ed) *Capitalism, Colonialism and Globalization: Studies in Economic Change*, Delhi, Tulika
Schofield, R. (1981) 'British population: change 1700–1871', in Floud, R. and McCloskey, D.N. (eds) *The Economic History of Britain Since 1700, vol.1 1700–1860*, Cambridge, Cambridge University Press
Slicher van Bath, B.H. (1963) *The Agrarian History of Western Europe A.D. 650–1800*, London, Edward Arnold
Turner, M.E., Beckett, J.V. and Afton, B. (2001) *Farm Production in England, 1700–1914*, Cambridge, Cambridge University Press
Yotopoulos, P.A. (1985) 'Middle-income classes and food crises: the 'new' food-feed competition', *Economic Development and Cultural Change*, 33:3

Annex – Part 1

Table A1 Population of England and Wales and of Britain, constant prices GDP and agricultural output value 1701–1801

Populations in millions

Year	E+W Lee & Schofield	A Index	E+W Maddison	B Index	E+W+S Maddison	C Index	GDP £ million	Agricultural output value £ million
1701	5.29	100	5.632	100	6.673	100	50	20
1711	5.51	104.2	5.92	105.1	7.008	105	53.9	20.6
1721	5.66	107	6.222	110.5	7.361	110.3	57.5	24.1
1731	5.59	105.7	6.541	116.1	7.731	115.85	58.7	23.6
1741	5.94	112.3	6.875	122.1	8.12	121.7	64.1	26.1
1751	6.2	117.2	7.227	128.3	8.528	127.8	70.4	28.1
1761	6.62	125.1	7.596	134.9	8.957	134.2	81.9	28.9
1771	6.97	131.8	7.985	141.8	9.408	141	80.3	29
1781	7.57	143.1	8.393	149	9.881	148.1	82	31.5
1791	8.21	155.2	8.822	156.6	10.378	155.5	104.1	33.4
1801	9.16	173.2	9.277	164.7	10.902	163.4	135.8	36.2

Note: Agricultural output and GDP in million pounds, population in millions.

Source: Cole 1981, for GDP and agricultural output value in constant 1700 prices. Schofield 1981, for population estimates. Chambers and Minday 1970 for estimated 43 per cent rise in cereal output during 1700 to 1800, which has been distributed over decades in the same proportion as agricultural output value. Maddison 2006 for alternative population estimates.

Table A2 Estimated index of total cereal output in volume units, and indices of per capita cereal output 1701-1801

	Per capita cereal output index		
Cereal output	A	B	C
100	100	100	100
101.6	97.5	96.7	96.8
110.9	103.6	100.4	100.5
109.6	103.7	94.4	94.6
116.2	103.5	95.2	95.5
121.5	103.7	94.7	95
123.7	98.9	91.7	92.2
123.9	89.7	87.4	87.9
130.6	91.3	87.7	88.2
135.6	87.4	86.6	87.2
143.4	82.6	86.8	87.5

Note: Per capita cereal output under A, B, C is calculated using the three population series A, B, C in Table A1.

PART 1

Figure A1 Indices of total cereal output and per capita cereal output 1700-1800

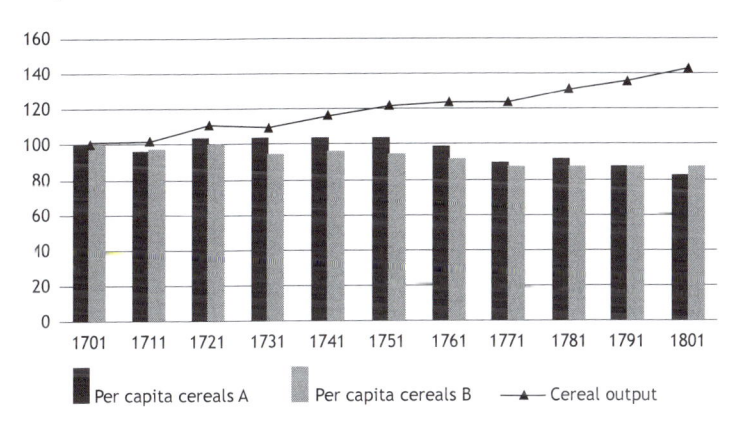

Source: Table 1a in Patnaik 2011

Figure A2 Indices of population, total cereal output and per capita output 1700-1800

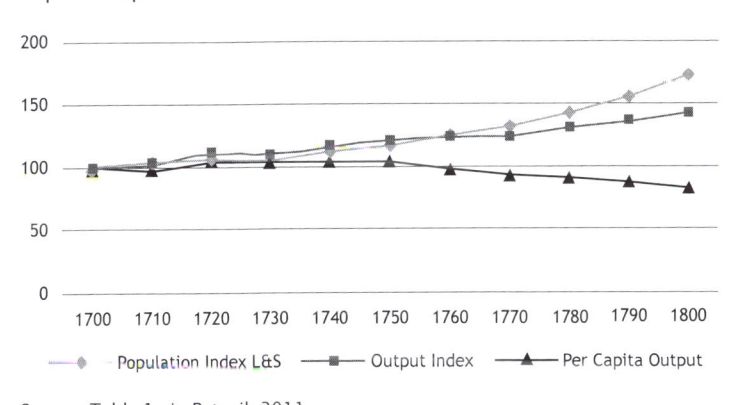

Source: Table 1a in Patnaik 2011.

59

THE AGRARIAN QUESTION IN THE NEOLIBERAL ERA

Table A3 Gross and net output of corn (wheat) selected years England and Wales 1700-1850

Gross and net output of wheat in England+Wales
In million bushels

	E+W Wheat acres million	Average yield bushel/acre	Gross output million bushel	Gross output million quarters	Seed bushel/acre	Seed million bushel	Net output million bushel
1700	1.752	19.07	33.41	66.82	2.4	4.21	29.2
1750	1.7	22.42	38.11	76.22	2.4	4.08	34.03
1800	2.19	20.98	45.94	91.88	2.7	5.91	40.03
1820	2.55	23.6	60.18	120.36	2.7	6.89	53.29
1850	3.42	27.47	93.95	187.89	1.6	5.47	88.48

Source: Turner, Beckett and Afton (2001) Ch 7, Table 7.1

Table A4 Annual per capita output of wheat, England and Wales, in bushels and in kilograms

	Net output million bushel	Net output million kg	Population million	Per capita kg
1700	29.2	743.53	5.29	140.55
1750	34.03	866.218	6.2	139.71
1800	40.03	1019.2	9.16	111.27
1820	53.29	1356.47	12.071	112.37
1850	88.48	2252.22	17.603	127.95

Source: Net output from Table 2a in Patnaik 2011, population from Schofield 1981

Note: 1 quarter = 28 pounds, 1 bushel = 2 quarters of wheat (corn) = 56 pounds. The bushel is a volume measure and the weight of different crops per bushel will vary, and of wheat will vary depending on moisture content. On average one bushel (imperial measure) of wheat with standard moisture content weighs 56 pounds or 25.45kg. The conversion from bushels to kilograms above has been made on this basis to allow comparison with present-day grain output and availability. Population for 1701, 1801 and so on is shown against output for 1700, 1800 and so on.

Part 2
Primitive accumulation and the destruction of African peasantries

Sam Moyo

8 Introduction: a failed agrarian transition in Africa

Fifty years after Africa's decolonisation most African peasants persistently face a crisis of social reproduction, manifested in food insecurity and malnutrition. Post-independence Africa failed to resolve the basic agrarian questions of improving agricultural productivity (Mafeje 2003), improving the supplies of wage foods and providing raw materials for basic industrial and employment development (Patnaik 2003), and promoting accumulation from below. This failure obtains in the semi-industrialised peripheral states (such as South Africa, which retains its racially unequal structures), in the putatively 'successful' agrarian economies (e.g. Kenya, Malawi) and the fragile pastoral regions (Moyo 2010). Varied modes of African colonisation had entailed different strategies of capitalist penetration and agrarian surplus extraction, including accumulation by dispossession, expressed in different sub-regional trajectories of a failed agrarian transition.

Land dispossession was historically more extensive in southern Africa than in non-settler Africa, where the extraction of surplus value entailed the systemic exploitation of peasant labour engaged in export commodity production, leading to mal-integration, through the unequal world trade regime (Amin 1974). During the 1990s structural adjustment intensified Africa's agricultural extroversion and unequal extraction of surplus value, alongside a second but diffuse and low intensity wave of land concentration. Neoliberal food security policies led to increased food imports and food aid dependency (Moyo 2010). More recently there have been pervasive efforts by foreign capital to dispossess the African peasantry of their best lands and water resources, as well as to exploit peasant labour as 'outgrowers' and 'contracted farmers'

(Moyo 2011). The underdevelopment of Africa's agrarian production systems continues to reflect their subordination to monopoly finance capital.

Current agricultural policy reforms neglect the social reproduction requirements of African peasantries and pastoralists, ironically using the food deficits to justify the current land grabbing and create large-scale farms (Collier and Dercon 2009) in collaboration with African governments and capitalists (Moyo 2008). New forms of resistance and agrarian resource conflicts are emerging, including against increased foreign control of African minerals and oil resources. This long-drawn process of accumulation by dispossession and super-exploitation of labour (Moyo forthcoming) has its parallels elsewhere, as elucidated by Utsa Patnaik (see Part 1).

9 Primitive accumulation by dispossession in colonial Africa[1]

Africa of the labour reserves (Amin 1972) or 'settler Africa' (mainly South Africa, Rhodesia, Namibia, Kenya, Algeria, etc) had by the 1960s witnessed the first African wave of extensive land grabbing by European settlers. Settler colonial states created large-scale commercial farming systems based on private property rights. These were assigned mainly on individual family-operated farms, which were spatially segregated from the black African communal areas, and included some enclaves of agro-industrial estates, which were subsidised by the state. African peasants' land dispossession by the British South Africa Company and others led to widespread displacement and landlessness, which ensured the super-exploitation of cheap labour (compelled economically and otherwise), while destroying the peasant economies. Settler estates were also created in the lusophone territories (Mozambique and Angola), and on a smaller scale in various migrant labour 'sending' states (e.g. Malawi, Zambia, Mozambique). While these developments did not lead to the complete dispossession of peasant lands, such dispossession was extensive enough to undermine the peasantry (almost completely in South Africa), leading to the creation of a migrant labour system is southern Africa. This resulted not in 'enclavity', but a functional dualism which subjugated labour while repressing peasant farming.

Accumulation from above through land dispossession and displacement of the peasantry, and through economic and extra-economic coercion of labour in former settler-colonial countries, epitomised the first wave of alienation in southern Africa, from the 18th century until mid-1900. Given a veneer of legality by the British crown, European settlement led to monopolistic control over national water resources and public infrastructural investments. This control was buttressed by the dominant white settler ideology and state–society relations which were defined by the policies of racially discriminatory private property rights and state investments that favoured the large-scale farms while undermining the remaining peasants through discriminatory commodity markets. This shifted the production of food from peasants towards large farmers producing wage-food commodities that were supported by state marketing boards and European merchants. This mode of accumulation and political rule by the southern African state, including its institutions of taxation and social security, was racially discriminatory, undemocratic and repressive (Mkandawire 2011). This placed the burden of social reproduction on underpaid labour and the peasantries, in a subsidy on capital.

In non-settler Africa, two broad land alienation histories prevailed through an indirect mode of colonial rule (Amin 1972, Mamdani 1996). In 'Africa of the concessions' (largely in central Africa), land alienation by European trading and mining companies led to the creation of a few significant enclaves formed around agricultural plantations, with rudimentary agro-processing facilities, as well as raw mineral extraction enclaves. The mode of primitive accumulation entailed raw material plunder and limited infrastructural investments. The pedigree of resistance to this enclave dispossession, for instance in Cameroon, is well documented (Baye and Khan forthcoming).

Elsewhere, in Africa of the *'économia de traite'* (Amin 1974), which evolved from two centuries of European mercantilism, there was widespread African resistance to Lord Lugard's attempts to alienate land in West Africa (Mamdani 1996). This led to the pervasive growth of 'petty (agricultural) commodity production', among differentiated peasantries (Bernstein 2002) or 'small cultivators' (Mafeje 2003). This mode of colonisation also entailed institutionalised labour migration (albeit not backed by land alienation), including the incorporation of migrant farmers from northern territories of West Africa into the coastal and forest regions' economies. This led to the creation of diverse peasantries, including independent lineage family producers, farming labour

65

tenancies and various forms of sharecropping arrangements (Amanor 2008). Smaller-scale agricultural estates (e.g. for palm oil) also emerged in various countries. Nonetheless, the pockets of semi-feudal agrarian structures persisted (e.g. Northern Nigeria, Ethiopia) and/or were created under colonial rule (e.g. Uganda). This colonialisation matrix brought diversity to Africa's agrarian transition in relation to land alienation, production structures, labour relations and patterns of largely extroverted and disarticulated accumulation (Amin 1974).

10 Primitive accumulation and expanded reproduction?

In general from the 1960s, post-independence governments halted the pace of primitive accumulation through land alienation (Shivji 2009) by nationalising colonially alienated lands and creating state-derived leasehold land-tenure systems on remaining estates. This restricted foreign land ownership and also slowed down the commodification of agricultural lands. Most colonial efforts to create freehold private property regimes were stalled, although they were sustained in some countries (e.g. Côte d'Ivoire and Kenya) (Kanyinga 2000). Most independence governments abolished the exploitative labour regimes by rescinding poll taxes and other farming taxes, and by reversing the institutionalised labour migration systems. Moreover, armed struggles in Mozambique and Angola culminated in substantial land redistribution, although this was inadequate in countries such as Kenya and Zimbabwe (until 2000).

Independent states sought to promote expanded reproduction among the peasantry and new large-scale farms. From the 1970s the 'modernisation' of agriculture was largely pursued through bi-modal farming strategies, which sought to nurture middle and larger scale capitalist agricultural production systems alongside peasant subsistence farming. The large-scale farming comprised a few state and privately owned estates, some inherited nationalised colonial agricultural estates (e.g. in Tanzania, Malawi), and others created through land redistribution (e.g. in Kenya) or alienation of customary lands (e.g. Botswana, Malawi). This diverted national resources away from the peasantries, although a degree of productivity growth was promoted among peasants.

The dual objective of agrarian reforms in such states was to 1) enable state accumulation from agricultural surplus values, and 2) deepen the extroverted focus of African agriculture by expanding export cropping in order to increase foreign exchange earnings so as to pay for a growing import substitution industrialisation (ISI) process. State marketing boards and input support programmes were the channels used to extract substantial shares of the agrarian surpluses, purportedly for various national industries and other 'development' schemes (Shivji 2009). Yet, even national agrarian capitalists were subordinated to the extraction of surplus value by transnational agribusiness corporations, which were protected by centralised state marketing regulations. Surplus extraction continued to be at the expense of the superexploitation of African peasantries (Shivji 2009), and through the cheap labour provided to large estates.

After being admonished by the World Bank (through the Berg Report 1981) for failed agricultural experiments, agrarian policy bias (largely an urban bias), the putative inefficiencies of state interventions (e.g. trade protectionism, state marketing regulations and participation through commodity boards), and inefficient state farming (Mkandawire and Saludo 1999), the state retreated from subsidising agriculture.

From 1990 surprisingly similar national land policies were formulated in numerous countries (Manji 2006; UNECA 2004) on the back of the privatisation of state agricultural estates. Simultaneously, numerous domestic capitalist farming elites procured, or 'grabbed', middle-sized farm lands, and a few foreign capitalist farmers and corporations established large farms in some African countries (e.g. South Africans in Mozambique and South Africa), putatively in pursuit of expanding (traditional and) non-traditional exports (Moyo 2008). Countries such as Mozambique, Tanzania and Zambia were now concessioning off peasant lands, reversing earlier land nationalisations, while Botswana, which after independence had redistributed some of its few white-owned large-scale commercial farms, was expanding its large-scale ranching by dispossessing pastoralists of their land and water resources (Molomo 2008). This second wave of land alienation led to land dispossession and the displacement of significant numbers of peasant families, albeit in more scattered and smaller enclaves than in the first colonial wave of land grabbing in settler Africa. This process was popularly resisted, including through armed rebellion, albeit unsuccessfully given the feeble response of the burgeoning national 'civil societies' (Moyo and Yeros 2005).

During the late 1990s and early 2000s the commodification of land, through the appropriation and conversion into private property of land held under customary tenure systems, was leading to new land markets, but largely in newer enclaves. The orthodox view was that the absence of clear tradable landed property rights limited tenure security, and constituted a barrier to agricultural investment and food security (Mighot-Adholla 1994). African countries pursued land tenure reforms as part of the package of trade liberalisation and of deregulating domestic markets and investment policies. African land-tenure systems, wrongly characterised as 'communal', insecure and 'unbankable', continue to be identified as an underlying obstacle to agricultural development or investment into technologies which intensify productivity. Allegedly, the systems undermine individual incentives and restrict the mobilisation of agricultural finance. Some African states sought to address this through formalising and individuating land tenures (titling), as well as establishing larger scale commercial farmers and, more recently, through initiatives to decentralise the governance of land (Amanor and Moyo 2008), although empirical evidence on the land tenure–investment constraint was poorly grounded (Mighot-Adholla 1994). Most of these tenure reforms collapsed.

Unequal land distribution, which had generally been conceived as a problem of former settler colonies (Mafeje 2003), was spreading elsewhere in Africa as the concentration of land holdings emerged incrementally over time, through piecemeal state expropriations of land, formal land markets and informal land sales and rentals, derived from internal social differentiation and state support (Moyo 2008). Land ownership inequities reflected growing class, gender and ethno-regional cleavages, as well as other power relations based on various social hierarchies, creating localised land 'scarcities' and landlessness (Kanyinga 2000, Kanyongolo

2005, Amanor 2008). Restricted access to land by small producers became a key obstacle to agricultural productivity growth and social reproduction.

By the turn of the 21st century, however, such unequal land distribution represented neither large-scale land alienation, nor widespread landlessness, nor full proletarianisation outside former settler colonial Africa, but a socially significant and diffuse structure of land concentration which, legitimated by national land policies, marginalised substantial sections of the peasantry. In settler Africa, extensive land expropriation and the systematic regulation of migrant labour, through organised recruitment and peasant taxation, was intended to set in motion a proletarianisation process in the entire southern Africa region (Arrighi 1973), but it eventually amounted to a semi-proletarianisation process (Sibanda 1988, Moyo and Yeros 2005), especially in South Africa's neighbouring countries, which constituted its regional periphery. The multiple social costs of expanding large-scale and plantation farming, besides land alienation, included depressed labour and income regimes, malnutrition and the marginalisation of the urban poor and peasants. Three decades of neoliberal policies entrenched this system, as land redistribution was limited, until Zimbabwe's fast-track land reform in the 2000s (Moyo 2011).

The adoption of structural adjustment programmes, widespread in virtually all African countries by 1990, not only rolled back state protection of land rights and state support to the peasantry, it also imposed a food-security policy framework which reversed previous preoccupations with enhancing national food self-sufficiency based on national production, claiming that a market-based process would be 'accommodative' of national and household food supplies and access processes (Kalibwani 2005). Countries were exhorted to produce their own food only if they could do so 'efficiently', and they were not allowed to spend on storing food, since they could import food as and when needed. Keeping grain reserves was considered an 'irrational' cost, since monies would be kept aside to procure the required food. Many countries drained their public grain reserves. A number of countries were considered to have a 'comparative advantage' in producing traditional and new exports, on which they should focus instead. Peasant families were encouraged to diversify their means of securing income or cash (through farm and non-farm livelihoods) to procure food, with only the capable small farmers encouraged to produce their own food and sell surpluses to 'net food buyers'. Imports were considered price competitive and less costly for national budgets, although this bloated government indebtedness (see also World Bank 2008).

In the event, this policy undermined food production growth in Africa and led to escalating food insecurity, although the availability of adequate food at the national level was achieved in a few countries, during non-drought seasons. Household access to food for many was impossible on the market, while a few 'vulnerable' social groups were provided with 'targeted' food aid. Unsurprisingly, large-scale and better-off small farmers, who dominated the production and sale of domestic food, increasingly shifted towards agricultural exports, and national food imports increased. Access to food increasingly reflected class-based income inequalities (Mkandawire and Matlosa 1993), exacerbated in the mid-2000s by the so-called food-price crisis.

The anti-developmental stance of African agrarian policies undermined the capacity of the small producers and the state to deepen technological transformation, while overall structural adjustment policies led to income deflation through wage repression and reduced public expenditure, particularly in rural areas (to below 5 per cent of their budgets), and the raising of food and farm input prices relative to wages (Patnaik 2008). Indeed, the state retreated from financing credit, or the marketing infrastructure, from subsidising inputs or supporting technology generation and extension, as well as from financing various non-agricultural props for agricultural production and consumption, such as rural development and social welfare (consumption) transfers to the poor. The inadequacy of public investments in rural and agricultural infrastructure, such as irrigation, rural transport and bulk food storage facilities, and in ancillary services such as electricity, placed a critical constraint on the capacity of peasants to expand the production of and access to food. This, alongside trade liberalisation, reduced the purchasing power of the poor and restricted multipliers such as employment and incomes, leading to repressed local demand for peasant produce and farm inputs (Patnaik 2008).

Continued mal-integration into the unequal relations of the world capitalist system, including through unequal trade relations, thus entrenched domestic inequities and a crisis of peasant social reproduction (Shivji 2009). The recent crisis of capitalism, including the volatility of and increases in the world food and inputs prices, has served to deepen the dispossession and super-exploitation of millions of African peasants.

11 Recent land grabs and subordination of peasantries

A major reaction of capital to the recent food price crisis has been a new scramble for land in Africa, mainly to produce food and biofuels for export, using the large estate production model (Moyo 2008). At least five million hectares have been concessioned to foreign 'investors' in over 20 African countries (von Braun and Meinzen-Dick 2009, Cotula et al 2009, Thompson 2008, Tabb 2008). The large-scale land acquisitions through leasing and outright purchases by foreign capital in various African countries have escalated during the 2000s (GRAIN 2009), with the explicit and tacit approval of governments and sections of the elite in particular (Alden Wily 2008). This represents a third wave of land alienation in all the African regions, creating numerous enclaves of large plantations or estate farming, frequently alongside perimetric buffer zones of coopted small outgrowers.

A new scramble over African lands for agriculture, mining and natural resource extraction, entailing a growing East–West–South rivalry to gain footholds on the entire continent, is predicted (Yoros 2011). The land investors hail from as far afield as the US and various European countries, the Gulf states, China, South Korea and Brazil (GRAIN 2009). This trend raises concerns about not only the extent of land alienation and concentration, but also the potential intensified subordination of the continent's peasantry and labour by monopoly capital during the present crisis.

Indeed, most of the former settler African countries in southern Africa have encountered this as a third wave of large-scale foreign land acquisitions (or grabbing) and 'investments' in agriculture, in a process which builds upon already substantively privatised land tenure regimes, racially skewed land ownership and extensive social exclusion. The critical difference is that it is mainly previously alienated large-scale farmlands (owned by private and public corporations and individual white large-scale commercial farmers) that are being sold and/or leased out to additional foreign investors. The agrarian accumulation model continues to be based on an outward-looking agricultural strategy, except in Zimbabwe, which is veering towards internal markets, food sovereignty and autonomous development.

Social movements warn of a spectre of extensive dispossession and displacement of small farm producers and pastoralists (GRAIN 2009), although some civil society technocracies consider that these investments hold developmental opportunities and argue that the potential threat of dispossession can be mediated through internationally supervised guidelines on 'best practice'.

Some attribute these land acquisitions to a benign search for food security among countries destabilised by the world food price crisis, which peaked around 2005, and to agriculture's putative profitability to investment funds (von Braun and Meinzen-Dick 2009). Others glorify the green motives of such capital exports in search of allegedly clean fuels. It is also claimed that these foreign investments are an opportunity to reverse the stagnation of agricultural productivity and food insecurity in Africa (World Bank 2010, Cotula et al 2009), and that they are necessary to re-orient Africa's growth trajectory and to save the 'bottom billion' (Collier 2007). Yet, land alienation in favour of agribusiness is primarily extroverted towards the production of new exports, such as biofuel, food grains, timber and tourism, which alongside the mining concessions are at the expense of the needs of existing social networks of poor and middle peasant households. These discourses underplayed alternate endogenous agrarian reforms towards accumulation from below.

The current land grabbing is also justified by tendentious claims that there is abundant and unutilised land and natural resources, which are presumed to have no (formal) owners (von Braun and Meinzen-Dick 2009). Such land alienation builds upon long-standing colonial era attempts to reform agricultural lands, natural resources and tenure system by establishing private property rights and land markets, which are considered the *sine qua non* of agricultural investment. Indeed, the neoliberal land policy reforms unleashed during the 1990s had resuscitated the land commodification agenda and laid the legal and political basis for the current wave of land alienation.

This recent food 'supply problem' is thus being addressed through expanding agribusiness food production activities, including area expansion in the South, and the displacement of small food-producers. These processes further divert financial and related resources away from small producers (Patnaik 2008, Tabb 2008). Most international financial and food aid institutions seek increased aid monies to lend to the food-crisis-ridden and riot-stricken poor countries for grain imports, as well as to finance more food aid. This would increase imports from the West, alongside cash transfers to the poor to buy food from abroad and from local surplus areas. Rather than mobilise financial aid and truly concessional loans to support small farmers to increase food production in the South, this strategy would augment and re-finance agribusiness's dominance of food production and entrench the intensive capital-energy food system. For instance, consumers in the SADC region remain captive to food and inputs prices set in South Africa, and provide malnourished cheap labour to the South African and the region's enclaves. This represents a form of mal-integration into a dysfunctional global food system, based on the over-consumption of fossil fuel energy and speculative behaviour, which undermines the universal right to food.

Besides land grabbing the persistent strategy during the current crisis of capitalism is to deepen the incorporation of African peasantries into the world agricultural exports chain. The recent 'philanthropic' initiatives of the Alliance for Green Revolution in Africa (AGRA) purport, for instance, to support small farmers' agricultural productivity growth through the scientific generation of improved seeds in 16 African food crops and to improve marketing through access to inputs and through expanding their access to private credit and 'agro-dealers' (ActionAid 2009). This strategy is embedded into capital's technological and commodity monopolies because it includes the monopolistic generation of hybrid and genetically modified seed technologies rather than their mass generation at fair cost by and for small producers. This market-led strategy for promoting peasant productivity by supporting small farmers' production systems cannot reverse the systemic sources of agrarian de-accumulation, given the states' limited capacities to regulate agrarian capital and reverse unequal agrarian trade relations,. Instead, this 'peasant-friendly', market-based green revolution deepens the peasantries' subordination to the world agribusiness oligopolies.

It has also become evident that ecological imperialism and the effects of the North-driven climate change agenda are increasingly being marshalled against agrarian accumulation from below. The introduction through aid of carbon trading measures seeks to put more African land and biodiversity under external control, leading to the further displacement of peasantries. Already, climate change could limit the size of maize growing areas in the SADC region (RHVP 2007), while the region's preparedness for the anticipated effects of climate change is limited. The suggested adaptations could entail the relocation of peasants to areas with the agro-ecological potential to produce food. The construction of new infrastructures and technologies adapted to reducing growing seasons in some areas and their increase elsewhere in relation to water losses and gains are a prerequisite. This promises the continued marginalisation of peasants, while public investment in agrarian adaptation remains limited.

Recent mainstream debates on Africa's failed agrarian transition, its so-called agricultural and food crises, tended to narrowly attribute them to Africa's presumed ecological limitations, land tenure deficiencies and the putative technological backwardness of peasant producers (Collier and Dercon 2009). These debates have neglected to consider the effects of land alienation, the super-exploitation of labour (Shivji 2009), the result of unequal trade relations (Amin 1974), or the absence of positive agrarian policy interventions such as are found in the North. The longer term historical process of land dispossession and surplus value extraction, which limits industrial and agricultural productivity growth and has been prevalent since the advent of colonial state transfers of resources from the South, is illogically used to argue that African farming should follow its supposed 'comparative advantage'. This fallacy is fully exposed by Utsa Patnaik (see Part 1 of this volume).

Trade liberalisation, unfair competition with subsidised imports and the speculative manipulation of agricultural commodity markets have destroyed various productive industrial and agricultural activities in Africa. The increased production and importation of elite consumer goods, at the expense of locally produced 'traditional' goods, reinforces this disarticulation (Patnaik 2008), leading to further deindustrialisation and high unemployment levels in Africa. Meanwhile, income deflation arose from 'a secular shift in terms of trade against petty producers of primary commodities' (especially of peasants' food and export crops), through monopoly capital's pricing practices, and in relation to their oligarchic control of agricultural commodity markets (Patnaik 2008: 7). African farmers had in general already been exposed to global competition from heavily subsidised farmers in the North (ActionAid 2007) and exports were and are subjected to punitive non-tariff barriers (Ng and Yeats 1996). The net result has been wage recession and income deflation, leading to the compression of domestic agricultural demand during the 1990s. This was exacerbated in the 2000s by the world food crisis.

The world food system, which is itself a deeply integrated and oligopolistic agro-industrial complex, had for long survived a real-terms decline in food prices, based on subsidised food overproduction in the West (Tabb 2008), amid repressed food consumption and production in the South (Patnaik 2003). The recent real increase in oil prices has triggered the shifts in the uses of food to produce agrofuels, which has influenced increases in the prices of land. Continued trade protectionism, subsidised exports and imposed structural adjustments, which are propped up by the food aid system, were key to repressed food production in the South.

The use of food for agrofuel production and oil-related increases in farm inputs prices, however, were critical to the food price escalation (Ghosh 2008); they accounted for 85 per cent of the increases, despite being the proximate causes of the price escalation. The agrofuels production process is influenced by the political pressures and security concerns of the western energy industry, capital funds, the science and technology industry and the aid system, reflecting high levels of rent seeking strategies, led by professional lobbies and think tanks (von Braun and Meinzen-Dick 2009), as well as the so-called bureaucratic stasis and distorted incentives that drive aid officials (Bird et al 2003). The underlying driver, however, was finance capital's speculation in oil and other commodities (Tabb 2008, Ghosh 2008), including futures, which led to pricing commodities regardless of their actual physical supply and consumption. Wider systemic mechanisms drove the underproduction of food in the South and the related food price increases, given that the global food system is embedded in financial and commodity markets.

Indeed, the recent export of capital to Africa for the exploitation of agricultural land, water, minerals and other natural resources reflects the escalation of capital's speculative tendency to accumulate by dispossession, in the wake of the collapse of the housing, energy and secondary financial markets. The effects of the long crises of the oligopolistic capitalist system (Tabb 2008, Ghosh 2008, Patnaik 2008, Moyo 2010) have been to undermine the African peasantry and agriculture in general and depress social and food consumption in particular. Rather than enhance the participation of the majority of small producers, African agrarian reforms mainly seek commodity market and land tenure reforms, which deepen the continent's integration into the unequal world food system, exposing it to the current land grabbing.

12 Alternatives during the neoliberal crisis

The continued marginalisation of African agrarian systems and the dispossession of the peasantry can only be reversed by national and regional policies that seek food sovereignty by protecting land rights and access to water and by controlling biodiversity resources in favour of the peasantry. However, radical responses to land alienation, the food crisis and the demise of the peasantry in Africa that are not donor led are few, while the activism of social movements has in general failed to reverse land dispossession. Popular responses, particularly resistance to the inequitable grabbing of land, such as land occupations and other forms of struggle for access to resources, are mostly isolated and localised, although some are gaining momentum (Moyo and Yeros 2005, Patel forthcoming).

Rebuilding the African peasantry is a key front of resistance to the ongoing primitive and wider capitalist accumulation that is happening to the detriment of Africa's agrarian transition. Its production is based on self-employed family labour and wage remittances on family-owned lands, with the purpose of providing foods and other products primarily for self-consumption. In some cases, peasantries have been resilient, even under structural adjustment policies and through various world commodity price crises, even though their outputs have been insufficient (Mafeje 2003). During the crisis they continue to mobilise family and other kinship labour, nurture biological (seed) and other local resources, and adopt new crops and technologies (especially locally adapted ones) in order to expand low energy-intensive agricultural production for their social reproduction (Mafeje 2003), despite the withdrawal of state support and the persistence of unfavourable terms of trade.

A few recent agrarian reforms have broken with Bretton Woods' advice to promote market-based agricultural productivity growth and land reform. In Malawi, the state's input subsidy programme led to peasants expanding staple grain production, even though this benefited agribusiness input suppliers. Alongside this, the expropriatory land reforms in Zimbabwe have led to extensive land distribution and deep structural change in agrarian relations (Moyo 2011, Scoones et al 2010). However, both efforts remain tied into the neoliberal policy framework, in which dominant monopoly finance capital drives supplies of agricultural seeds, technologies and credit, at the expense of auto-centric development.

The required alternative prioritises food sovereignty and the sustainable use of resources by autonomous small producers in a system where democracy is inclusive and substantive and based on social progress. Alternative developmental approaches to agrarian transformation will require policies that direct the choice of agricultural commodities produced for social gains, supported by the (re)distribution of the means of food production (particularly of land, but also inputs such as seeds and water). Increased state social investments in the peasantry's social wellbeing is critical to systemic rural development, which includes enhancing the human resources of the peasantry, restructuring the national food system and improving endogenous research and extension capacities under the guidance of popular consumer trade protection and farmers' movements.

New regional integration strategies based on holistic agrarian reforms and aimed at collectively reversing the decline of domestic food production and food consumption, including protection from external shocks and dependency, are crucial. These have to counter the current market-based functional regionalism by building a popular regional industrial policy framework that systematically reverses the current opening up of the region (through trade and monetary harmonisation), which has reinforced the mal-integration of Africa into the global economy. The autonomous generation of sustainable agricultural technologies and the increased domestic supply of inputs that are focused on domestic food and local industries are essential to counter the dominance of monopoly finance capital in agricultural commodity and input markets, as well as over land. Food sovereignty requires policies which defend the African peasantry's land rights and the internal home markets.

13 Conclusion

Africa's failed agrarian transition primarily concerns the failure to produce adequate food for consumption by its urban and rural working peoples, and to provide raw materials for protected domestic and regional industries. This arises from its extroverted agricultural production and the unequal agricultural trade, which emanate from mal-integration into speculative world markets dominated by monopoly finance capital. The failed agrarian transition has emerged from long-term processes of primitive accumulation by dispossession and displacement, and the super-exploitation of labour through foregone consumption. Increasingly, this process is conveyed through the entry of various pliant emerging powers, such as South African capital in the southern African region. Through these, transnational agribusinesses dominate agricultural (land, inputs and outputs) and food markets in the name of investment under neoliberal conditionalities.

The protection of the largely peasant food production systems and the consumption needs of working peoples can only be achieved through collective regional food sovereignty and equitable regional development strategies, rather than alternative responses which reinforce the incorporation of the peasantry into volatile world markets and extend land alienation, while increasing import dependence. Otherwise, the scramble for Africa and primitive accumulation will persist through various forms of capitalist penetration. These include the increased supermarketisation of African food distribution systems by retail and farm input monopolies and the concessioning of land for the production of food, sugar and agrofuels for export by transnational capital from the West, East and South.

Note – Part 2

1. A more detailed account of these processes is presented in Sam Moyo 'Rebuilding African Peasantries: inalienability of land rights and collective food sovereignty in Southern Africa?' a CODESRIA/CRN project

References – Part 2

ActionAid (2007) 'The World Bank and agriculture: a critical review of the World Bank's World Development Report', London, ActionAid
—— (2009) 'Assessing the Alliance for the Green Revolution in Africa', Johannesburg, ActionAid International
Alden Wily, L. (2008) 'Whose land is it? Commons and conflict states: why the ownership of the commons matters in making and keeping peace', Washington DC, Rights and Resources Initiative
Amanor, K. (2008) 'Sustainable development, corporate accumulation and community expropriation: land and natural resources in West Africa', in Amanor, K.S. and Moyo, S. (eds) *Land and Sustainable Development in Africa*, London and New York, Zed Books
Amanor, K.S. and Moyo, S. (eds) (2008) *Land and Sustainable Development in Africa*, London and New York, Zed Books
Amin, S. (1972) *Neocolonialism in West Africa*, Harmondsworth, Penguin
—— (1974) *Unequal Development*, New York, Monthly Review Press
Arrighi, G. (1973) 'International corporations, labour aristocracies, and economic development in tropical Africa', in Arrighi, G. and Saul, J. (eds) *Essays on the Political Economy of Africa*, New York, Monthly Review Press
Baye, F.M. and Khan, S.A. (forthcoming) 'Land-tenure arrangements, migrant labour and land struggles in rural Cameroon', in Moyo, S., Tsikata, D. and Diop, Y. (eds) *Land in the Struggle for Citizenship in Africa*, Dakar, CODESRIA Multinational Working Group (MWG)
Berg, R. (1981) 'Accelerated Development in Sub-Saharan Africa: An Agenda for Action', Washington DC, World Bank
Bernstein, H. (2002) 'Agrarian reform after developmentalism?', presentation at the Conference on Agrarian Reform and Rural Development: Taking Stock, Social Research Centre of the American University in Cairo, 14–15 October 2001
Bird, K., Booth, D. and Pratt, N. (2003) 'The contribution of politics, policy failures and bad governance to food security crisis in southern Africa', paper commissioned by the Forum for Food Security in Southern Africa, http://www.odi.org.uk/work/projects/03-food-security-forum/docs/PolProcesses_theme1.pdf, accessed 28 July 2008
Collier, P. (2007) *The Bottom Billion: Why the Poorest Countries are Failing and What Can Be Done about It*, New York, Oxford University Press
Collier, P. and Dercon, S. (2009) 'African agriculture in 50 years: smallholders in a rapidly changing world', FAO Expert Meeting on How to Feed the World in 2050, 24–26 June

Cotula, L., Vermeulen, S., Leonard, R. and Keeley, J. (2009) *Land Grab or Development Opportunity? Agricultural Investment and International Land Deals in Africa*, London, International Institute for Environment and Development (IIED), Food and Agriculture Organisation of the United Nations (FAO) and International Fund for Agricultural Development (IFAD)

Ghosh, J. (2008) 'The global oil price story', International Development Economic Associates (IDEAs), www.networkideas.org/jul2008/news28_oil_price.htm, accessed 6 April 2011

GRAIN (2009) 'Grabbing land for food', *Seedling*, January

Kalibwani (2005) 'Food security in Southern Africa: current status, key policy processes and key players at regional level', paper for the 'Promoting the use of CSO evidence in policies for food security: an action research project in southern Africa', ODI/SARPN/FANPRAN, October

Kanyinga, K. (2000) 'Re-distribution from above. The politics of land rights and squatting in coastal Kenya. A report from the research programme "The political and Social Context of Structural Adjustment in Africa"', research report 115, Uppsala, Nordic Africa Institute

Kanyongolo, F. E. (2005) 'Land occupations in Malawi: challenging the neoliberal legal order' in Moyo, S. and Yeros, P. (eds) *Reclaiming the Land: The Resurgence of Rural Movements in Africa, Asia and Latin America*, London, Zed Books

Mafeje, A. (2003) 'The agrarian question, access to land and peasant responses in sub-Sahara Africa', *Civil Society and Social Movements Programme Paper 6*, Geneva,

Mamdani, M. (1996) Citizens and Subjects: Contemporary Africa and the Legacy of Late Colonialism, Princeton, NJ, Princeton University Press

Manji, A. (2006) The Politics of Land Reform in Africa: Form Communal Tenure to Free Markets, London and New York, Zed Books

Mighot-Adholla, S.E. (1994) 'Land, security of tenure and productivity in Ghana', in Bruce, J.W. and Migot-Adholla, S.E. (eds) *Searching for Land Tenure Security in Africa*, Dubuque, Kendall/Hunt Publishing Company

Mkandawire, T. (2011) 'On tax efforts and colonial heritage in Africa', *Journal of Development Studies*, 46: 1647–69

Mkandawire, R. and Matlosa, K. (eds) (1993) *Food Policy and Agriculture in Southern Africa*, Harare, SAPES Books

Mkandawire, T. and Soludo, C. (1999) *Our Continent, Our Future: African Perspectives on Structural Adjustment*, Dakar, Ottawa and Asmara, CODESRIA, IDRC and AWP

Molomo, M.G. (2008) 'Sustainable development, ecotourism, national minorities and land in Bostwana', in Kojo S.A. and Moyo, S. (eds) *Land and Sustainable Development in Africa*, London, Zed Books

Moyo, S. (2008) African Land Questions, Agrarian Transitions and the State: Contradictions of Neoliberal Land Reforms, Dakar, CODESRIA

Moyo, S. (2010) 'Agrarian question and the developmental state in southern Africa', in Edigheji, O. (ed) *Constructing a Democratic Developmental State in South Africa: Potentials and Challenges*, Cape Town, HSRC Press

Moyo, S. (2011) 'Land concentration and accumulation by dispossession: redistributive reform in post-settler Zimbabwe', *Journal of Agrarian Change*
—— (forthcoming) 'Rebuilding African peasantries: inalienability of land rights and collective food sovereignty in southern Africa?', CODESRIA/ Comparative Research Networks

Moyo, S. and Yeros, P. (2005) 'The resurgence of rural movements under neoliberalism', in Moyo, S. and Yeros, P. (eds) *Reclaiming the Land: The Resurgence of Rural Movements in Africa, Asia and Latin America*, London, Zed Books

Ng, F. and Yeats, A. (1996) 'Open economies work better! Did Africa's protectionist policies cause its marginalization in world trade?', *World Bank Working Paper*, 1636

Patnaik P. (2008) 'The accumulation process in the period of globalisation', 28 May, www.networkideas.org/focus/may 2008/fo28_globalisation.htm, accessed 26 April 2011

Patnaik, U. (2003) 'Global capitalism, deflation and agrarian crisis in developing countries', *Journal of Agrarian Change*, 3(1–2): 33–66

Patel, R. (forthcoming) 'Electing land questions: a methodological discussion with reference to Abahlali baseMjondolo, the Durban Shackdweller Movement', in Moyo, S., Tsikata, D. and Diop, Y. (eds) *Land in the Struggle for Citizenship in Africa*, Dakar, CODESRIA Multinational Working Group (MWG).

Regional Hunger Vulnerability Programme (RHVP) (2007) 'Bio-fuel production and the threat to South Africa's food security', *Wahenga Brief*, 11

Scoones, I., Marongwe, N., Mavedzenge, B., Murimbarimba, F., Mahenehene, J. and Sukume, C. (2010) *Zimbabwe's Land Reform: Myths and Realities*, Harare, Johannesburg and Oxford, Weaver Press, Jacana Media and James Currey.

Shivji, I.G. (2009) *Accumulation in an African Periphery: A Theoretical Framework*, Dar es Salaam, Mkuki na Nyota Publishers

Sibanda, A. (1988) 'The political situation', in Stoneman, C. (ed) *Zimbabwe's Prospects: Issues of Race, Class, State and Capital in Southern Africa*, London and Basingstoke, Macmillan

Tabb, W.K. (2008) 'The global food crisis and what has capitalism to do with it', 18 July, http://www.networkideas.org/feathm/jul2008/ft18_Global_ Food_Crisis.htm, accessed 26 April 2011

Thompson, C. (2008) 'Bio-fuels for Africa?', revised paper (6 May 2008) for National Consultative Workshop on Current Issues affecting Agro-Biodiversity for Civil Society Positions to CBD-COP9, Norton, Zimbabwe, 28–30 April 2008

United Nations Economic Commission for Africa (UNECA) (2004) *Assessing Regional Integration in Africa. ECA Policy Research Report*, Addis Ababa, UNECA

von Braun, J. and Meinzen-Dick, R. (2009) ' "Land grabbing" by foreign investors in developing countries: risks and opportunities', *IFPRI Policy*

Brief 13, Washington DC, International Food Policy Research Institute (IFPRI)

World Bank (2008) World Development Report 2008: Agriculture for Development, Washington DC, World Bank

World Bank (2010) Rising Global Interest in Farmland: *Can it Yield Sustainable and Equitable Benefits?*, Washington DC, World Bank

Yeros, P. (2011) 'Reclaiming Africa: scramble and resistance in the global crisis', concept note

Index

Africa
    agrarian transition 62–3, 81
        alternatives 79–80
        land tenure systems, perception 69
        rebuilding of peasantries 79
Africa Company 15
Africa, expanded reproduction 67–72
    agrarian policies 67–8, 71–2
    land alienation 1, 68–9
    post-independence changes 67
    structural adjustment programmes 70–1
    unequal land distribution 69–70
Africa, land dispossession
    agrofuel production 77–8
    alternatives 79–80
    capitalist speculation 78
    colonialisation matrix 4, 66
    ecological issues 76–7
    justification 74–5
    non-settler alienation 65–6
    settler estates 64–5
    third-wave acquisitions 1–2, 73–4
    world agribusiness oligopolies, subordination to 75–6
    see also land dispossession, southern countries
agrarian crisis
    1924–25 9
    India 10
    neoliberal era, issues 10–11
agrarian transition, Africa *see* Africa, agrarian transition
agricultural revolutions, internal 14
agriculture, corporatisation 51–2
agrofuel production 77–8

Alliance for a Green Revolution in Africa (AGRA) 2, 75
Australia, land productivity 32, 33

Bereano, P.L. 2
Berg Report 68
Bidwells Agribusiness 1
Bretton Woods institutions 10, 79–80
Britain
    population growth (18th cent.) 20, 57 *Table*
    Treasury 9, 10
Brownlee, J. 20
Bush, George 44

calorie intake, per capita 36, 37 *Table*
capitalism
    acquisitive actions 3–5, 16–17
    instability 48–9
    speculation effect 78
    see also neoliberal policies
cereal consumption 44, 45 *Table*, 46
    China 44
    England *see* English agricultural revolution, wheat
    negative income elasticity of cereal demand 41–2
    see also foodgrain decline
cereal output
    China 39, 41
    English agricultural revolution 20–3, 26, 58 *Table*, 60 *Table*
    see also English agricultural revolution, wheat
    northern countries 39
    southern countries 39
    see also foodgrain decline

INDEX

Chambers, J.D. 20, 21
China
    cereal consumption 44
    cereal output 39, 41
    as emerging country 3
    land productivity 17, 18
Cole, W.A. 20
colonisation 47
comparative advantage theory
    (Ricardo's) 11, 28–33
    basic argument 28
    England/Portugal example 28, 29
    fallacies in argument 28–9
    land productivity 17–18, 32–3
    mutual benefit assumption 29–32
contradictions analysis 50–1
Corn Laws repeal 24, 26
corporatisation of agriculture 51–2

decolonisation 47
displacement land accumulation 49

East India Company 15
economie de traité 65
emerging countries 3
encroachment/displacement land
    accumulation 49
English agricultural revolution 20–7
    cereal output 20–3, 26, 58 *Table*,
        61 *Table*
    free food imports agitation 26
    import dependence 26–7
    wheat
        imports 23–5, 24 *Table*, 25
            Fig., 26
        output 60 *Table*
        output/consumption 22–3
English, T.M. 2
Ethiopia 1
expanded reproduction *see* Africa,
    expanded reproduction
export specialisation 37–9, 40

fallacy types 29 *Fig.*
feed demand rise 42–3
finance capital 3
food
    for export 1–2
    security 34–41
foodgrain decline 41–6
    cereal consumption 44, 45 *Table*,
        46
    feed demand rise 42–3
    free trade cost 41–6
    grain cost as direct/indirect
        determinant 43–4, 43 *Fig.*
    income distribution effects 46
    negative income elasticity of
        cereal demand 41–2
    per capita, India 34
    see also cereal consumption;
        cereal output
free trade cost 34–46
free trade cost *see under* foodgrain
    decline
free trade cost
    export specialisation 37–9, 40
    food security 34–41

Gates Foundation 2
GDP, per capita decline 10
genetically modified (GM) seeds/
    inputs 2, 51
Ghana 1
global primary product prices 10
grain cost as direct/indirect
    determinant 43–4, 43 *Fig.*
great depression, inter-war 9–10
Green revolution 2

income distribution effects 46
India
    agrarian crisis 10
    cereal consumption 44, 46
    as emerging country 3

87

foodgrain, per capita 34
Green revolution 2
income distribution effect 46
land productivity 18, 32
Industrial Revolution 26

Kalecki, M. 9
Keynes, J.M. 9, 41
Krugman, Paul 44, 46

land dispossession
　southern countries 11–12, 50–3
　see also Africa, land dispossession
land productivity, north/south
　comparisons 17–18, 32–3
land question 47–9
　capital inflows 48
　capitalist instability 48–9
　colonisation/decolonisation 47
　contradictions analysis 50–1
　corporatisation 51–3
　encroachment/displacement
　　accumulation 49
Lee and Schofield series 20, 21
Lewis, W.A. 17, 18, 31–2, 32
Libya 3
Lugard, Lord 65

Madagascar 1
Maddison, A. 20
Malawi 80
Mali 1
Marxism 3
Mexico 2
militarisation, inter-war 9–10
Mingay, G.E. 20, 21
monopoly trading companies 15

National Sample Survey (NSS) 46
negative income elasticity of cereal
　demand 41–2
neoliberal policies
　effects 8–9

great depression, inter-war 9–10
　pillars 8
　see also capitalism
Nigeria, land productivity 32, 33
northern countries
　acquisitive actions 16–17
　cereal output 39
　food consumption 14–15
　import dependence 26–7
　primary sector production 14
　see also southern countries
Nyerere, Mwalimu Julius 8

Overton, M. 21–2

peasantry
　Africa
　　rebuilding of 79
　　see also Africa, land
　　　dispossession
　dispossession 11–12, 50–3
Portugal 28
primary products
　global prices 10
　import dependence 26–7
　mutual benefit assumption 29–32
　north/south comparison 15, 16
　　Table
　northern countries 14–15
primitive accumulation, Africa see
　Africa, agrarian transition; Africa,
　land dispossession

Ricardo, David
　Corn Laws repeal 26
　theory see comparative advantage
　　theory

Schofield, R. 20, 21
Slicher van Bath, B.H. 14
Smith, Adam 43
South Africa Company 64
South Korea 3

INDEX

South Sea Company 15
southern countries
   cereal output 39
   land dispossession 11–12, 50–3
   tropical biodiversity 36
   see also northern countries
sub-Saharan Africa
   calorie intake, per capita 36, 37 *Table*
   food staples, per capita 34, 35 *Table*, 36
Sudan 1

thrift paradox 41
tribal resources, dispossession 50–3
tropical biodiversity 36

UN Food and Agriculture Organisation 42

United States
   Federal Reserve 10
   land productivity 18
USAID 2

West Africa 65–6
wheat
   Britain *see* English agricultural revolution, wheat, imports
   see also cereal consumption; cereal output
World Bank 68

Yotopoulos, Pan 44

Zimbabwe 80